Preventing and Managing
Workplace Bullying and Harassment

A RISK MANAGEMENT APPROACH

Moira Jenkins, PhD

AUSTRALIANACADEMIC**PRESS**

First published in 2013 by Australian Academic Press
Level 5, Toowong Tower, — 9 Sherwood Road,
Toowong QLD 4066, Australia
www.australianacademicpress.com.au

National Library of Australia Cataloguing-in-Publication entry:

Author:	Jenkins, Moira, author.
Title:	Preventing and managing workplace bullying and harassment : a risk management approach / Moira Jenkins, Phd.
ISBN:	9781922117113 (paperback) 9781922117120 (ebook)
Subjects:	Bullying in the workplace.
	Conflict management.

Dewey Number: 658.3145

Disclaimer: This book is intended as a guide only. While the author endeavours to
provide accurate and current information, she is unable to provide legal advice to
you, your organisation or employees, and you are encouraged to obtain independent
legal advice to verify the accuracy, currency or completeness of any information
contained in this book. The author is not responsible for any adverse consequences
resulting from the use of any recommendations, ideas contained in this book.

Book and cover design by Maria Biaggini — The Letter Tree.
Image by ©istockphoto/A-digit.

TESTIMONIALS

"An essential book for anyone interested in this critical workplace issue, written by someone who genuinely knows her stuff."
— *James Adonis, Business Writer, Fairfax Media.*

"Moira's approach to workplace bullying is realistic, practical and well-informed. She deals with the complexities and ambiguities in bullying through a comprehensive and well written text. Ideal for HR Practitioners, small business owners and OH&S professionals who want to improve their practice. This is a really good book!"
— *Charlotte Rayner. Professor of Human Resource Management, Portsmouth Business School, UK.*

"This book presents a unique combination of findings from the scientific literature, the organisational and legal landscape in Australia, and the author's extensive professional experience. It offers clear practical guidelines that managers and workers will find invaluable to help them deal with and prevent bullying and harassment at work."
— *Professor Helen Winefield, School of Psychology, University of Adelaide, South Australia.*

"Enhances the ability of managers and employers to avoid some of costly and tragic consequences of bullying and harassment in the workplace and provide them with the confidence to respond appropriately should these issues arise in their workplace."

— Amanda Rishworth M.P., Chair of the House of Representatives Education and Employment Standing Committe Federal Member for Kingston

"Moves beyond a simplistic approach of trying to solve bullying by focusing solely on the individuals involved. Instead, Moira utilises over a decade of research to provide guidance from a perspective that addresses not only individual behaviours, but the background risks that contribute to the behaviour. This is a useful and practical guide for all professionals who are interested in preventing and managing workplace bullying."

— Karl Luke, Partner, Thomsons Lawyers

CONTENTS

PART 1
INTRODUCING BULLYING AND HARASSMENT

PART 2
ASSESSING THE RISKS

PROLOGUE

Like any hazard in the workplace, bullying constitutes a significant threat to the health, safety and welfare of employees. Bullying also has financial and legal implications for employers including poor productivity, low morale, increased absenteeism and staff turnover all which contribute to increased costs and loss of profits. The legal costs in defending bullying and harassment cases can be significant, and the publicity that often accompanies high profile cases contributes to negative exposure for both organisations and individuals.

Modern Australian safety law has its origins in early 1970s England with the introduction of the *Health and Safety at Work Act 1974*. This Act was the most important development in industrial safety legislation for many years. It introduced a new approach to health and safety with emphasis on self-regulation and employee participation. Prior this, the approach to industrial safety had been based on legislation that had grown in a piece-meal fashion over the last 100 years. Acts of Parliament were passed and extended to deal with particular hazards and work activities as they arose. Despite the vast amount of legislation, millions of workers were not covered by law in the course of their employment and there was no statutory provision for the protection of the public. In 1970 the British Government set up a committee, chaired by Lord Robens to review the situation. The Robens report was published in June 1972. The report's fundamental conclusion was

> 'There are severe practical limits on the extent to which progressively better standards of safety and health at work can be brought about through negative regulation by external agencies. We need a more effectively self-regulating system. This calls for the acceptance and exercise of appropriate responsibility at all levels within industry and commerce. It calls for better systems of safety organisation, for more management initiative and for more involvement of work people themselves'.

It was from this report that modern health and safety laws came into being. Today, these laws require employers to ensure 'so far as is reasonably practicable' the health, safety and welfare of their employees and other persons who may be affected by their work. The fundamental need for employer's to take responsibility for health and safety of their workers is now enshrined in all Australian safety laws. The key message for employers is to be proactive in health and safety, and consult extensively with the workforce. This is the cornerstone of the occupational health and safety approach to dealing with workplace bullying.

As a lawyer practicing in the area of employment, safety and workers compensation law for over 20 years, I have seen bullying and harassment become an increasing issue of concern, as good employers recognise the importance of having a safe workplace free from the risks associated with these psychological hazards. In more recent times, legislators have become more active in passing laws placing an onus on employers to do all that is reasonably practicable to ensure their employees are not exposed to certain kinds of inappropriate behaviour. In the health and safety law context, there is an increasing recognition that bullying is a psychological hazard that has the potential to cause significant damage not only to individuals but also to the workplace more generally. Legal avenues have opened for affected individuals to make claims against employers for damages for breach of statutory duty and at common law as well as for employers to be prosecuted under relevant safety laws. However, despite these significant legal risks and increasing awareness of the often devastating effect of workplace bullying and sexual harassment, many employers continue to find it difficult to address the issue, and are inevitably 'reactive' rather than 'proactive'. This is often due to lack of knowledge about what needs to be done prevent bullying and harassment from occurring, and when it does occur how to address it promptly and effectively.

Despite the potential legal consequences that may be imposed, many employers are largely unaware of their legal responsibilities and worse still unsure what steps to take to reduce or eliminate the risk of bullying in the workplace.

Moira Jenkins book '*Preventing and Managing Workplace Bullying and Harassment: A Risk Management Approach*' provides the necessary tools that allow employers to identify psychological hazards in the workplace and to put in place risk controls to eliminate or at least minimize risks to health and safety. These measures are part of an employer's legal responsibilities to do everything that is reasonably practical to prevent bullying and harassment occurring.

This book presents the reader with a practical, evidence based guide to preventing and managing workplace bullying and harassment from within this occupational health and safety framework. Through her extensive research, and experience as a psychologist, mediator and conflict coach, Moira has understood the importance of engagement with the workforce. She has applied this knowledge and experience to the development of practical and applied ways of preventing and managing bullying and harassment.

The first part of the book introduces the concept of workplace bullying, and how bullying and other forms of workplace harassment can contribute to psychological injuries. Through a number of case studies Moira highlights how the workplace environment allows bullying to develop and escalate, often with devastating results. The second and third parts of the book describe in practical and easily applied terms how to take a risk management approach to preventing workplace bullying. This includes how to consult with employees and other parties to identify risks within the organisation and develop strategies that need to be taken to control and manage these risks. The forth section of the book describes a number of approaches to address bullying and harassment should it emerge as a problem. Rather than focusing solely on the target and perpetrator, Moira's approach highlights the need to also address bullying from a systemic perspective and take into account the factors in the workplace that contributed to the emergence and development of the behaviour.

This book is to be applauded for moving beyond a simplistic approach of trying to solve bullying by focusing solely on the individuals involved. Instead, Moira utilises over a decade of research to provide guidance on preventing and managing workplace bullying and harassment from a perspective that addresses not only individual behaviours, but the background risks that contribute to the behaviour. This is a useful and practical guide for all professionals who are interested in preventing and managing workplace bullying from an evidence based framework.

Karl Luke, partner at Thomsons Lawyers

FOREWORD

Workplace bullying and harassment is one of the most significant workplace and health and safety issues of our time. It can occur in any business big or small, in the public or private sector, and in any industry. Workplace bullying and harassment can be overt such as yelling or insulting a person, or covert such as deliberately excluding, isolating or marginalising a person in workplace. The impact of workplace bullying is significant not only the individual who is being bullied or harassed but to other employees who witness the behaviour and the wider organisation.

Workplace bullying and harassment causes significant damage. As the Chair of the House of Representatives Standing Committee on Education and Employment's recent inquiry into workplace bullying, I heard first hand of the damage both physical and psychosocial caused to individuals as a result of workplace bullying and harassment. This included depression, post traumatic stress disorder, anxiety, insomnia, and in some of the worst cases suicide. However workplace bullying and harassment does not only affect individuals, it impacts on the whole workplace or organisation. The Productivity Commission estimates that workplace bullying costs the Australian economy between $6 billion to $36 billion annually. Costs to business include expenses associated with staff turnover, recruitment costs, sick leave, workers compensation; time spent by management on resolving issues and complaints, as well as general loss of workplace productivity.

While it is evident that workplace bullying and harassment can have a negative toll on both the individual and businesses, many workplaces have seemed reluctant to address the issue, and importantly, implement measures to prevent it. This may be because workplace bullying is complex and circumstances can be sensitive as they involve conflict between people. However, the evidence is clear that negative workplace culture can lead to, or exacerbate workplace bullying and harassment. Therefore addressing and preventing workplace bullying is not only the responsibility individuals but also the responsibility of organisations and businesses. Evidence presented to the House of Representatives Standing Committee's inquiry was clear that an organisation's culture and the presence or absence of prevention strategies have a critical impact on the incidence of workplace bullying and harassment.

It is for this reason that workplace bullying and harassment should be viewed as an occupational health and safety issues. As a result, prevention should be seen as an important goal where organisations aim to manage risk and put controls in place to minimise injury. For many workplaces, it may take a significant mind shift to see workplace bullying and harassment from this perspective. While it easy for workplaces to identify need for a guard on a piece of machinery, it can be more difficult when managing their human resources. Despite the added complexity, preventing psychosocial injury should be seen as no less important. Assisting workplaces to make this shift is critical if we are going to seriously tackle workplace bullying and harassment in Australia.

That is why Dr Jenkins' book *Preventing and Managing Workplace Bullying and Harassment: A Risk Management Approach* is so important and indeed timely. In this book Dr Jenkins provides straightforward and practical advice to help workplaces tackle bullying and harassment. This resource will assist employers and mangers to implement strategies that can prevent and manage issues of workplace bullying and harassment. Though using an Occupational Health and Safety perspective, the book provides constructive advice on how organisations, managers, supervisors, human resource personnel and occupational health and safety representatives can understand, assess, identify and manage risks that could lead to, or exacerbate bullying and harassment in the workplace.

Dr Jenkins draws on her years of experience working as a psychologist, conciliator, mediator and trainer in the area of workplace bullying and harassment to put together this useful and practical resource that is easy to understand. This book includes many case studies and examples from the real world, as well as examples of tools such as a climate surveys that could be used by workplaces to gather important information about workplace culture. Importantly, it provides advice to managers when dealing with issues of workplace bullying harassment such as, when to and when not to use mediation to resolve an issue.

Preventing and Managing Workplace Bullying and Harassment: A Risk Management Approach will enhance the ability of managers and employers to prevent incidences of bullying and harassment as well as provide them with the confidence to respond appropriately should these issues arise in their workplace. By implementing this approach businesses and organisations can avoid some of costly and tragic consequences of bullying and harassment in the workplace.

Amanda Rishworkth M.P.
Chair of the House of Representatives Education and Employment Standing Committee Enquiry into Workplace Bullying. Federal member for Kingston.

ACKNOWLEDGEMENTS

This book could not have been written without the support and assistance of a number of colleagues and friends who generously gave advice when I needed it, read early drafts of this manuscript and gave me much needed encouragement when times were tough. I would sincerely like to thank Robert and Alanagh for trusting me with their stories. Thank you to Bette Phillips for your assistance. A big thank you goes to Declan Fahie, Carlo Caponecchia, Karl Luke, Vicki Knott and Oonagh Barron for reviewing drafts of the manuscript and providing valuable and helpful feedback. I would also like to thank each person who participated in my earlier doctorial research. I have used some of your stories to illustrate important aspects of his book. I have changed your names, and some identifying features to protect your anonymity, but you all know who you are. Lastly, Thank you to Drew for your continuing support and patience. I could not have carried out this project without you.

PART 1

Introducing Bullying and Harassment

CHAPTER 1

What Is This Book About?

Preventing and managing workplace bullying and harassment, is not just a 'feel good' exercise, or something organisations should only do when they are faced with a complaint. It is part of core business, and employers and managers have a duty of care as part of occupational health and safety (OH&S) laws to prevent hazards that might contribute to workplace injuries. Bullying is a psychological hazard that can injure employees. Sexual, and other forms of harassment, while traditionally not examined through an OH&S framework also have the potential to contribute to psychological injuries. Employers need to prevent and manage these psychological hazards in the same way they would manage any other potential workplace hazard or safety matter.

International research indicates that generally between 1% and 4% of employees experience serious bullying, and between

8% and 10% have experienced minor bullying on at least a weekly basis.[1] However, up to 20% of employees are exposed to behaviour that while not reaching the threshold of bullying, is a severe workplace stress in itself.[2] This behaviour has the potential to develop into bullying if left unchecked. In a recent Australian survey of 800 employees across a number of occupations, More than 50% reported that they had witnessed bullying behaviour and over 25% said they had been had been a target of bullying. Poor management of the bullying was reported to be a major issue for survey respondents with only 30% of targets and less than 50% of witnesses, being satisfied with the way their organisations handled of the situation. More than 50% also noted the bullying behaviour had been going on for over 6 months[3].

If one takes the conservative amount of 2% to 3% of severe bullying that occurs in the workplace as reported in the international bullying literature[4], that means in an organisation employing around 1,000 staff, between 20 and 30 people may be being bullied at any point in time. As well as being a safety issue, bullying can have a significant effect on an organisation's bottom line. One of the first things employees do when faced with threatening and intimidating behaviour at work is stay home. Increased non-attendance, high staff turnover and reduced productivity, as well as possible workers' compensation claims and potential litigation, contribute to significant financial costs and are the economic reflections of misery. The Australian Human Rights Commission (AHRC) estimated that workplace bullying costs Australian employers between six and 36 billion dollars every year.[5]

By its nature, bullying as well as sexual harassment is an escalating process. When the situation reaches the stage where a worker who feels bullied or harassed lodges a formal complaint against a perpetrator, it is unlikely that the working can be restored. The investigation of a bullying and harassment complaint is often adversarial, with one party trying to prove they were bullied or sexually harassed, and the other party denying or justifying their behaviour. Investigations usually require witnesses to be interviewed, and team members are drawn into the investigation process, often taking sides. Meanwhile the organisation is hoping that news of the allegations will not be leaked to the press or that they will lead to legal action. The indirect costs of this decrease in production and increase in stress are often compounded with the direct costs of sick leave and workers' compensation claims. It makes good business sense to prevent bullying and harassment from occurring before an organisation receives a complaint.

Australian research into workplace bullying and harassment has been going on now for more than two decades, so we know that workplace hazards such as bullying and harassment to not occur 'out of the blue' but develop from an environment that is permissive of poor behaviours and is highly stressful. Just as a poor physical safety environment can expose employees physical risks leading to falls, burns and other physical injuries, an environment that is permissive of inappropriate behaviour, poor leadership behaviours and other workplace stressors can contribute to high levels of conflict, bullying, and sexual harassment.

Examining the work environment for risk factors that can contribute to bullying and harassment is the beginning of this OH&S approach. Characteristics of individuals, including the target and perpetrator, poorly managed change as well as the quality of the social interaction within a specific work group or the broader work environment itself, are all risk factors for bullying and harassment.[6] Other risk factors include the way work is organised, and the quality of leadership within the workplace.[7] A management style that is either laissez faire (so staff get away with inappropriate behaviours, and are poorly managed) or authoritarian, can be a risk to the development of bullying and harassing behaviours.[8,9] Bullying is more likely to occur in environments where workers perceive contradictory and unclear expectations from their manager.[10] Bullying and harassment is also more likely occur when workplace cultures or dynamics fail to accommodate the inherent differences present in a diverse workforce. In these workplaces some employees may be marginalised by the inflexible attitudes of managers, other employees, organisational processes or 'taken for granted' practices in the workgroup.[11] This can contribute to hostile workgroups, cultures and climates.

On an individual level, perpetrators of workplace bullying or harassment may act in an abrasive manner to protect their own self-esteem, lack social competencies or utilise bullying or discriminatory behaviours to improve their status within the organisation.[12] Other perpetrators may be motivated to maintain the 'norms' within the prevailing culture of the organisation, and therefore bully or harass targets who threaten those norms. Job insecurity is also linked with workplace bullying. However, a recent study suggests that bullies who *are more secure* in their job may be more likely to behave badly.[13] The researchers in this study found that the relationship between job insecurity and workplace bullying was stronger when the perpetrators reported that they very secure jobs. This suggests that perpetrators may be more likely to bully when the consequences of their behaviour is low (i.e., if they are able to get another job if they are fired, or they are not held accountable for their behaviour).

Workplace cultures and environments that are permissive of sexualised behaviours can also contribute to sexual harassment at work. Sexual harassment can occur independently of workplace bullying, though the behaviour can also be defined as bullying when the sexually suggestive behaviours are repeated and unwanted, and are a health and safety risk to the target. Sexual harassment also often occurs as part of a pattern of bullying, and many bullied workers such as the two you will meet in the case studies at the beginning of this book, describe sexually harassing and bullying behaviours occurring concurrently. Just as bullying can have a negative impact on a targets health and safety, sexual harassment too has the potential to cause significant psychological and/or physical injury.

It is more difficult for workplace bullying and harassment to develop when the risk factors that contribute to the emergence of this behaviour are identified, managed appropriately, and controlled. This book outlines a framework for identifying and managing these risks.

Part one of this book identifies the hazard. It explains what we mean by 'workplace bullying'. It examines the different types of bullying that can occur and highlights the overlap that exists between bullying, sexual harassment and unlawful discrimination. Part two describes how to implement a risk management approach. This needs to be carried out as part of a consultation process within the workplace, but this book will provide you with the tools to — (i) identify and assess the degree of risk within your organisation and (ii) take steps to control the risks that have been identified. Part three discusses what control measures an organisation needs to undertake to lessen the identified risks. Part four examines a number of actions employees can take when things go wrong, and a complaint of workplace bullying or harassment is received by human resources departments. The issues involved in mediating a complaint of bullying from within a risk management framework are outlined, and the issues organisations need to be mindful of when investigating a bullying complaint are discussed. Part five provides tips and tools specifically for targets, those individuals who might be responding to a complaint made against them, and human resources (HR) consultants who are managing a complaint.

Workplace Bullying: The Human Cost

Throughout this book, you will be introduced to individuals who have been experienced psychological injury through bullying and sexual harassment. These are real case studies based on real events. However the names of the individuals involved and the identifying features of the organisations have been changed to protect anonymity. It is hoped that by reading and reflecting on the case studies presented that you will come to understand a little more about the causes and effects of workplace bullying and harassment. These case studies illustrate the complex and very human dimension of bullying and harassment, and underscore why a preventative risk management approach to this hazardous behaviour is so important.

While the individual perpetrators in the stories that you will read about, all bear responsibility for their behaviour, they were only able to behave badly for as long as they did, because witnesses didn't speak up and because key people failed to take appropriate action. When reading these stories, rather than focusing on the specific bullying and harassing behaviours, try to identify the features of the workplace that you think contributed to the behaviour, or allowed it to escalate. Some of these features include characteristics of the target that made them vulnerable, styles of management that contributed to the bad behaviour, or allowed the behaviour to escalate unchecked, as well as the way the organisation responded to the allegations.

Mick's Story

Mick is married to Vicki and they have four adult sons. Mick cracks jokes and laughs easily. He also cries easily. He said that prior to seeing me today, he thought he was going to be sick and was very anxious. However, it was important for him to tell his story, so that others know what can go wrong when people are bullied, sexually harassed or treated badly at work. He also felt that it was important for employers to understand what can happen when complaints aren't taken seriously or dealt with properly.

Prior to being employed by the organisation where the allegations of bullying and sexual harassment took place, Mick had previously operated his own successful business'. He left this business to take up the offer of a contract position within a particular organisation. He said:

> I was initially called in to the organisation because they had a lot of staff leaving and needed some help. I had been doing some contract work for them, and initially I started with a short term four week position, but that one month revolved into a year and a half. Eventually, they created a permanent position for me.

Mick had been working for about nine months, when a new manager was appointed to his section. He said:

> I wasn't particularly interested [in the position] and didn't even apply for it. The previous manager had resigned and left because of his own issues with management, and I had been on my own for about five months before they appointed this new manager. It was a month later I put in my first complaint.

He said that within the first couple of weeks of the new manager being appointed, he started to exhibit 'bizarre behaviour' in the office.

> He started to rub around the area where his penis is, and his overall behaviour was erratic to the extreme. At nine o clock, we might be in a meeting in his office where he would lie back in his chair, rubbing his groin, talking about some of the females in [the] organisation. At ten o'clock, he would be raving in the extreme, using explicit language about his own manager. At 11 o clock, he could not remember any decisions we had agreed to at the meeting two hours earlier. He was also very, very technically challenged, and I think he felt very insecure in his actual technical abilities and threatened by me, never mind his emotional instability ... I was on a conference call with him one day. As I took my turn to speak with [the person on the other end of the phone], he pushed back in his

chair, pushed his tongue in and out repeatedly and rubbed over his private area. There were other things that he was doing, and there were lots of volatile encounters. I refer to them in that way because he was known to fly off the handle in a big way. When I say 'fly off the handle', I mean his whole face would distort, and he would yell at you, flay his hands and throw things. All you could do is stand back and think, 'bloody hell — there is something wrong with this dude'.

One day our senior manager walked past and said, 'How is the new guy going?' I told him then that there were some issues, but I also said, 'You have a real problem because he plays with himself'. He said, 'What do you mean?' And so I explained, and that was the moment in time that changed my life because weeks went by and nothing happened. This guy kept rubbing himself, and this was on top of his poor technical abilities and management style, and so I began putting in regular complaints. I was in the senior manager's office a minimum of once a week and saying whatever you are doing [to stop the behaviour] is not working. He is now doing this or that … he's now grabbing bits of wood and pretending to masturbate and doing all sorts of stuff. His behaviour continued and got worse, and I generally was able to walk away, but following a particularly explosive encounter … I lost it myself … Let's just say that I was somewhat controlled but I really flew off the handle. I was very upset and angry, and had had enough of his behaviour … and I went into his office and lost it. I used the foulest language I ever have, and I just let him know what I think, and I slammed the door. I am surprised I didn't break anything. About half an hour later, he came into my office and said, What are you up to?' 'Do you fancy a cup of tea? It was like the incident we had just had, never even occurred. I went again and told the senior manager what had happened, and the senior manager took us both out for a coffee. Basically, he [the alleged perpetrator] denied everything, and so the senior manager said, 'if you two guys don't sort this out amongst yourselves, one of you will have to go'. And so I shut up about it for a while,. I didn't want to lose my job.

Mick told me that the sexually inappropriate behaviours and the bullying continued for around two years. He and two other staff members then submitted a written complaint as directed by the organisations complaint procedure for bullying and harassment. However, before submitting this written complaint, Mick said:

> I had been to the director dozens multiplied by 20 times. Not only the director, but what they called 'bullying and sexual harassment contact officers'. I went to HR. I remember going to HR in the early days, and that's when I heard that there had been other complaints about his behaviour. But HR said they weren't acted on because 'the girls didn't want to put it in writing ...' So unbeknown to me at the time, females had already been to HR. I also went over to the department that is meant to oversee ours and talked to HR there. The person I spoke to said, 'We got to get you out of there'. That was the common thread. My rebuke always was 'no there is no reason I have to leave'. I wanted it sorted. I didn't want to leave a job that I loved.

The written complaint of bullying and sexual harassment was signed by Mick and two other staff members who said that they had also been subjected to the specified behaviour. When they wrote up the complaint, the three complainants cut and pasted the organisation's definition of bullying from the policy and outlined the behaviours to which they were being subjected. Their complaint stated in part:

> We as a group declare that we all at some time or another have been subjected to most of the behaviours as stated. We further declare that these behaviours have been going on since [sic] and we now require assistance to resolve these issues ... Further to representations made to you last week we, the undersigned, want to bring particular issues to your attention.
> • intimidating aggressive body language
> • verbal threats
> • shouting and screaming
> • sexual and racial harassment
> • persistent nit-picking or unjustified criticisms

- isolating or ostracising an individual
- spreading gossip or rumours about a person
- creating extra work or disrupting a person's ability to work
- setting unreasonable deadlines
- withholding information from an employee so they are less able to do the job
- preventing access to opportunities
- humiliating an individual through sarcasm, criticism or insults, sometimes in front of other employees or customers
- threats or acts of physical violence
- sabotage of a person's work
- constant surveillance of an employee to a greater extent than others, with no justifiable reason.

We, as a group, declare that we all, at some time or another, have been subjected to most of the behaviours as listed. We further declare that these behaviours have been ongoing since [sic] and we now require assistance to resolve these issues.

Mick said that the organisation's response to the complaint was that management could not act on the allegations because the complainants were not specific enough about the alleged behaviours, so he provided the following clarification:

Sexual and Racial Harassment
Persistent references to Muslims and Catholics.

Persistent reference to how the Indonesians severed penises off of Dutch soldiers and rammed them down their throats.

References to the 'chopping off of heads of children' and the showing of pictures sent to him.

Persistent 'touching' around the private areas in front of staff in main work area, and in privacy of office in front of staff.

Persistent sexual lewdness with various objects around the office (anything resembling a penis).

Disrupting a Person's Work
Constantly in the main work area talking sex and general crap.

Humiliating an individual through sarcasm, criticism or insults, sometimes in front of other employees or customers.

Constant critical references to the likes of [sic] representatives and [sic] representatives about [sic].

Relentless criticism about [sic].

Persistent nit-picking or unjustified comments.

Constantly telling [sic] that he should not be so friendly with staff, and that he should not be having lunch with them, and that he is not a capable manager of people.

Constant enquiries as to what we were talking to other officers about.

Shouting and screaming and intimidating aggressive body language.

Various heated episodes with the project manager, [sic] and

Telling various staff that various individuals can 'get fucked', while remonstrating loudly with extreme body language.

Shortly after receiving his amended complaint with the clarification, Mick said that he received correspondence that in part said

You will no doubt be aware that I cannot act officially until I receive a formal complaint. I have been informed that only once during this period was a formal complaint laid and this resulted in a mediation session and counselling for those involved. It is my understanding that your approaches to various contact officers, peer support officers and management during this period were made informally and no official complaint was filed.

Mick said that he was becoming more and more anxious and upset with the behaviour to which he was being subjected. He was also becoming angry at the organisation's failure to act on his allegations despite numerous verbal and written complaints being made. He started having sleep problems, becoming very anxious to the point of wanting to vomit in the mornings before work and was intolerant of small things that would normally not bother him.

> Around this time, my doctor completed a medical certificate
> to attach to my WorkCover claim, a claim that cited sexual
> harassment and workplace bullying as the cause of my anxiety
> and depression. I was off for three months. It took many
> months for my claim to be approved as management was
> denying that I was being harassed or bullied.

However, about two months later, an independent investigation
into the allegations was commissioned. On his return to work,
Mick was moved out of the department and placed on a different
floor of the building where he felt isolated from the team and
given no work to do. He said he felt like a pariah and troublemaker, both for complaining and having had so much time off
work. He said that because of the way the organisation was treating him, he felt not only bullied by the individual perpetrator but
by the organisation as well. It was at this point that he decided to
make an external complaint of sexual harassment to the Anti-
Discrimination Commission. In his complaint, he alleged that the
organisation was responsible for behaviour that he was being subjected to because they failed to stop it, despite his many verbal
and written complaints.

While the complaint against the individual perpetrator was
resolved at a conciliation conference[14], Mick said that he was
unable to resolve the issue with the organisation, as he believed
that they were victimising him for making the complaint, and
were still not taking the issues seriously. Therefore, he took the
organisation to court. Mick said that after he complained he was
viewed by the organisation as a troublemaker, and he felt victimised for bringing the organisation into disrepute.

> There had been a lot of publicity regarding the trial, and my
> name was mud in the department.

At the time Mick made his complaint, the legal definition of
sexual harassment was very narrow. The State legislation has since
changed to widen the definition of sexual harassment making it
similar to the national definition under the Federal Sex

Discrimination Act. There was also a six-month time limitation on complaints, which meant that Mick needed to make a complaint no later than six months after the last act of sexual harassment. Unfortunately for Mick, he had complained six months and two weeks after the last act of sexual harassment. Therefore, his complaint did not met the legal definition of sexual harassment, was out of time, and the court did not find in his favour. However, in summing up, the judge said that had the sexual conduct described by Mick corresponded with the legal definition of sexual harassment under the legislation at that time, and had been within time, the organisation would have been vicariously liable for the behaviour. This is because they did nothing about Mick's complaints at first, and their responses were inadequate when they finally did act. In the court's view, the organisation 'implicitly authorised the conduct' by doing nothing about the complaints, or not doing sufficient about them.

Mick still sees a psychologist, and although he has managed to hold down two senior positions for a short time since leaving the organisation, he cannot manage normal work stressors or challenges. Despite his best efforts at controlling his emotions, he becomes teary easily, overreacts and becomes very anxious over small things. Owing to these ongoing levels of high anxiety and depression, he has been unemployed for the last three years.

I still have moments when I feel nauseous, and even doing volunteer work (which I am trying to do), I feel like throwing up when I am going into a workplace. I now live in a vicious cycle. I am still looking for work to support my family, but the closer I get to a job, the uglier the symptoms become. How do I explain away my absence from the workforce? How do I go through an interview while battling waves of nausea that just get more intense? I definitely keep away from crowds. I worry if I am asked to go to someone's house for dinner. I am embarrassed by my symptoms ... I remember that fateful day when I complained about my manager rubbing his groin in the office ... that's when my nightmare began. All management had to do was ... well, do something about it. But they didn't.

QUESTIONS TO PONDER

- What background variables in the organisation do you think contributed to the bullying and sexually harassing behaviours described by Mick? Why were they able to continue?
- How would you describe the management style within the organisation?
- Many HR consultants were aware of the allegations but did not act. What is the responsibility of an HR consultant in preventing and managing bullying and harassment?
- What should the director or chief executive have done to address the allegations?
- What is the difference between a 'formal' and 'informal' bullying complaint? Does a complaint have to be in writing before managers act?
- What happens when allegations are ignored?
- Was it worthwhile taking the complaint to court, given that it wasn't substantiated?
- What are some of the challenges in taking a complaint to court that are highlighted by Mick's story?

Stuart's Story

Stuart was almost 21 when he died. He had been working as an apprentice chef for just over two years. The bullying began the week that he started work. His mother described him as outgoing, happy, extroverted and popular boy who sometimes pushed the boundaries like any normal teenager. He played soccer and had a good network of friends. He was on top of the world. He was excited to have been accepted for the apprenticeship and talked about a future where he was able to do something that he loved.

Stuart lived at home with his parents and his two sisters, in a small town. A large organisation advertised for two apprentice chefs, and Stuart was really excited because he always wanted to be a chef. Apparently, there were over 70 applicants, but Stuart was one of the lucky two that were successful in obtaining the position. The other person was a girl who was also about the same age as Stuart; he was 16 and nine months on the day he started working. Unfortunately, the head chef, who was also the training officer, had wanted someone else to get the apprenticeship, but the kitchen manager, who worked above the head chef, had chosen Stuart.

It appeard to his mother that Stuart was treated badly right from when he began. When he first got the job, Stuart would come home and say things like he had to do the menial tasks for the whole week, while the other apprentice carried out a variety of tasks. His parent's just said to him that as an apprentice, you have to start at the bottom, and in time the duties that you both do should even themselves out. However, that didn't seem to happen.

On one occasion, Stuart said that he was called outside where the head chef was having a cigarette with another staff member. Stuart had with him a bucket of soup that he was transporting to another section of the organisation. The head chef apparently asked Stuart what sort of soup it was, and Stuart replied, 'beef and vegetable'. The head chef then kicked the bucket of soup over and said, 'Where is the f***king beef and vegetables', and made Stuart get a hose and clean up the mess. This was witnessed by a number of the staff, and Stuart felt really embarrassed. One of the people who witnessed this later said to Stuart that he shouldn't put up with that sort of behaviour and should complain, but Stuart was too frightened of the head chef to tell anyone. No one challenged the head chef's behaviour.

On another occasion the head chef asked Stuart to make some sandwiches — half brown and half white. Stuart was too anxious to ask for clarification, so he made the sandwiches with brown bread on top and white on the bottom and then was ridiculed for this in front of other staff members. He was told he should have made half a tray of white bread sandwiches and half a tray of brown bread sandwiches. However, by this time Stuart felt that no matter which way he had made the sandwiches, he would have been made to look like a fool. He felt that there was no way to please the head chef. Stuart often said that he couldn't do anything right.

Stuart also told his parents about the behaviour to which the other apprentice was being subjected. He said that the head chef was placing bets with other staff as to how long it would be before he had sex with her, and there was a running tally being kept. Stuart felt he could tell no one about what was happening at work. Everyone in the kitchen knew that the head chef was *really* the boss — not the kitchen manager.

The longer Stuart was there, the worse the behaviours that he was subjected to became. After a while, he started telling his parents about direct physical threats and inappropriate sexual behaviours that were occurring. After weekends, the head chef would publicly ask questions about his sexuality and started spreading rumours that he was a homosexual. Stuart told his mother that one day when he bent over to get something the head chef pushed his crotch into his backside and pretended he was having sex with him. Everyone in the kitchen thought this was funny. However, to a 17-year-old boy, it was embarrassing and scary. Another thing that Stuart told her was that every year the kitchen staff organised an overnight fishing trip for the male employees, and he was really looking forward to this. However, he didn't end up going because the head chef made a comment that frightened him. Stuart said that he was asked 'what will your mum do if you come home with blood up your arse and grass on your knees?' Stuart was intimidated and decided not to go on the fishing trip.

Stuart first complained about the behaviour during a routine visit by a representative of the training organisation that was overseeing his apprenticeship. He spoke to the representative about the bullying and sexual harassment but didn't go into great detail because he was embarrassed. However, he did tell the representative from the training organisation that the head chef was giving him a hard time. Later that day when he was back in the kitchen, he said that the head chef came up to him and said 'I hear I have been giving you a hard time Stewy'. The representative from the training organisation had told the head chef what Stuart had said. No action was taken at that time by the training organisation. As a consequence, the bullying continued.

At times, Stuart told his parents that things had improved and the head chef was treating him well. However, these times were always followed by worse incidents of bullying, causing confusion and a hope that things were improving. His parents felt that this was a form of game playing where the head chef would 'reel Stuart in' to give him a false sense of security so he could then abuse him again and get the maximum reaction.

On one occasion Stuart said that the head chef asked him to count two 2 kg bags of beans because he felt they (whoever sold them the beans) were ripping them off. Stuart was to write down how many beans were in each bag and work out the average. Stuart knew the head chef was trying to play a joke on him but was fearful of the repercussions if he did not follow his orders.

Sometime later, the other (female) apprentice had put in a complaint with the training organisation about the sexual harassment to which she was being subjected. In her complaint, she apparently named Stuart as a witness, saying that he had been subjected to even worse behaviour than she had. Because she had submitted a formal complaint, Stuart decided to make a formal complaint as well. During the investigation, Stuart continued to work with the head chef, but the organisation gave him a 'buddy' to go to at work if he had any problems. After submitting the complaint, Stuart had a few days off because he was too scared to go to work but reluctantly agreed to go back to work even though he was very nervous and frightened. At this stage, he wasn't sleeping and had started to smoke marijuana to help him cope with the stress. His parents could tell at home that he wasn't coping and was withdrawing from them and all of his friends. The head chef denied all of the allegations and instead said that Stuart was not performing well in his job, and the complaint was a reaction against him trying to manage Stuart's poor performance. Even though the complaint was substantiated, Stuart said there didn't seem to be any consequence for the head chef, as he kept working. Meanwhile, Stuart became more and more depressed while the behaviour at work continued in a less public and more subtle manner.

During this time, the female apprentice who had also complained was moved and placed in a different department within the organisation. However, Stuart continued to work in the kitchen with the head chef.

Stuart said the pressure of working became too much and he felt as though all the workers were talking about him. He began getting very paranoid at work and was more intimidated by the head chef because by now he was so anxious he had begun making silly mistakes and not asking for assistance when he really needed it. At home, his parents would tell him to 'hang in there' and the issues would be resolved soon.

One day his mother found Stuart was curled up in a foetal position in his bed crying and saying he couldn't go to work and couldn't cope anymore. The ongoing bullying and the lack of response from a second complaint contributed to him getting more depressed. He went to his doctor and was granted sick leave on WorkCover. He was not yet 19 years of age, and he was not coping very well. During this time, he ended up having three admissions to a psychiatric hospital due to psychotic episodes. He had begun self-harming and his anxiety had become so bad he was rarely leaving the house, no longer going out with friends. He was on antidepressant medication, but was also self-medicating with marijuana, which was making his anxiety worse. He was seeing a psychiatrist and a psychologist, and a number of other people were trying to help him. By this stage, Stuart was too sick to go to work. He was angry because he had been forced to leave (for medical reasons) a job that he loved, and from all that he knew, the head chef was not made to take responsibility for any of his behaviour, as he was continuing to work. He was also angry with the training organisation, and his host employer because he believed no one had taken his complaints seriously or followed through by stopping the head chef's behaviour. It seemed that *he* was the troublemaker by complaining, and now that he was no longer at work, it didn't matter how long the investigation took or what happened.

As well as the initial formal complaint, with his parents help, Stuart also lodged a complaint of sexual harassment with the Equal Opportunity Commission and that complaint was conciliated. However, by that stage he was too sick to go to work anymore, and was too scared to go back into the work environment. During the conciliation conference, the person who was supposed to be have been Stuarts support person at work following his first complaint, arrived at the conference as the head chef's support person. When Stuart saw this, he had a panic attack and completely shut down. He no longer trusted any of the staff, as none had spoken out about the behaviour and none had supported him. Even when Stuart was no longer at work but was on stress leave, it didn't seem to us that the organisation did anything to address the behaviours that contributed to Stuart becoming mentally unwell. It seemed that once he became ill, his illness became the focus rather than the reason he became ill in the first place. He became labelled as a troublemaker for complaining so much, and his use of marijuana became the focus on why he was suffering from mental health issues.

Twelve months after Stuart had ceased working at the kitchen, he and his mother made a complaint to the state OH&S regulator about the bullying and an investigation commenced. However, Stuart committed suicide before the investigation could be completed.

The coroner's initial report stated Stuart had had a fight with his girlfriend and subsequently killed himself. However, after taking into account the material presented to him by Stuart's mother, who requested he amend the finding, the report included the fact that Stuart had been suffering anxiety, depression and a posttraumatic stress disorder after alleged bullying.

QUESTIONS TO PONDER

- What background variables do you think contributed to the behaviours exhibited by the head chef being able to emerge and continue?
- How would you describe the management style within the organisation?
- Many people were aware of the behaviour and allegations but did not act. What are their various responsibilities?
- Who was responsible for stopping the bullying?
- Did Stuart's poor performance and mistakes at work justify the behaviour to which he was subjected? How should the organisation have managed the performance problems?
- What do you think should have occurred after the allegations in the initial formal complaint were substantiated?
- If the complainant is demonstrating behavioural difficulties and is known to be taking illicit drugs, should the organisation act on his/her allegations?
- What happens when allegations are ignored or minimised?

Endnotes

1 Zapf, D., Einarsen, S., Hoel, H. & Vartia, M. (2003). Empirical findings on bullying in the workplace. In S. Einarsen, H. Hoel, & C. Cooper (Eds.), *Bullying and emotional abuse in the workplace: International perspectives in research and practice* (pp. 103–126). London, England: Taylor and Francis.

2 Zapf, D., Escartin, J., Einarsen, S., Hoel, H., & Vartia, M. (2011). Empirical findings on prevalence and risk groups of bullying in the workplace. In S. Einarsen, H. Hoel, D. Zapf, & C. Cooper (Eds.), *Bullying and harassment in the workplace: Developments in theory, research and practice* (2nd ed., pp.75–107). London, England: CRC Press.

3 Drake International. (2009). Workplace bullying still rife in Australian companies. Retrieved from http://au.drakeintl.com/hr-news/hr-articles-publications/workplace-bullying-still-rife-in-australian-companies.aspx.

4 Zapf, D., Einarsen, S., Hoel, H., & Vartia, M. (2003). Empirical findings on bullying in the workplace. In S. Einarsen, H. Hoel, & C. Cooper (Eds.), *Bullying and emotional abuse in the workplace: International perspectives in research and practice* (pp. 103–126). London, England: Taylor and Francis.

5 Australian Human Rights Commission. (2004). *Workplace bullying. Fact sheet.* Retrieved from http://www.humanrights.gov.au/info_for_employers/fact/workplace.html

6 For example, Salin, D., & Hoel, H. (2011). Organisational causes of bullying. In S. Einarsen, H. Hoel, D. Zapf, & C. Cooper (Eds.) *Bullying and harassment in the workplace: Developments in theory, research and practice* (2nd ed., pp. 227–245). London, England: Taylor and Francis.

7 Leymann, H. (1996) The content and development of mobbing at work. *European Journal of Work and Organisational Psychology, 5,* 165–184.

8 O'Moore, M., & Lynch J. (2007) leadership, working environment and workplace bullying. *International Journal of Organisational Theory and Behaviour, 10,* 95–117

9 Vartia, M. (1996) The sources of bullying: Psychological work environment and organizational climate. *European Journal of Work and Organisational Psychology, 5,*(2), 203–214.

10 Bowling, N., & Beehr, T. (2006) Workplace harassment from the victims perspective: A theoretical model and meta-analysis. *Journal of Applied psychology, 91*(5) 998–1012.

11 Einarsen, S. (1999). The nature and causes of bullying at work. *International Journal of Manpower, 20*, 16–17.

12 Zapf, D., & Einarsen, S., (2011). Individual antecedents of bullying: Victims and perpetrators. In S, Einarsen, H. Hoel, D. Zapf, & C. Cooper (Eds.), *Bullying and harassment in the workplace: Development in Theory, Research and Practice* (2nd ed, pp. 177–200). Boca Raton, FL: CRC Press.

13 De Cuyper, N., Baillien, E., & De Witte, H. (2009). Job insecurity, perceived employability and targets' and perpetrators' experiences of workplace bullying. *Work and Stress, 23*(3), 206–224.

14 Conciliation is an alternative dispute resolution (ADR) process similar to mediation. The disputing parties with the assistance of a third person (the conciliator), sit down together with the aim of identifying the issues in dispute, developing options to resolve the complaint, and endeavour to reach an agreement. When sexual harassment and discrimination complaints are lodged with Equal Opportunity Commissions or Anti-Discrimination Commissions in Australia, one of the first steps in the process of resolving the complaint is through a conciliation process. This is a confidential process, and most complaints do not go to court because they are successfully resolved in this way.

CHAPTER 2

Identifying the Hazard

What Is Meant by 'Workplace Bullying'

Because the term 'bullying' is often a common expression for bad behaviours, there is considerable confusion as to what it actually is. The result of this confusion is that workers mistakenly believe that a single episode of inappropriate or threatening behaviour, a minor office dispute or disagreement, an altercation with a manager or unfavourable performance reviews are all examples of bullying. This means that organisations and regulatory authorities receive complaints labelled 'bullying' that are in fact, high levels of conflict rather than workplace bullying. For this reason, it is important for workers and managers to be aware of what bullying is, and what it is not. The use of bullying as a generic term for a number of conflicts and work-related disputes serves to undermine the seriousness of the impact of true workplace bullying, and the ability of organisations to monitor and prevent it from occurring. Bullying is NOT just workplace conflict, or personality clashes, or occasional rudeness or poor management decisions. Workplace bullying is *repeated unreasonable behaviour that specifically targets a person, or a group of people, and over time, contributes to the target/s becoming increasingly unwell.* Bullying is more than disrespectful behaviour and conflict. Bullying is repeated abusive behaviour.

To add to the confusion as to what behaviours constitute bullying, a number of different terms are used in the literature to describe what we know as work place bullying; for example:

• bullying
• mobbing
• harassment
• emotional abuse
• workplace incivility
• psychological harassment
• counterproductive workplace behaviour.

These different terms often are a reflection of where the bullying research was carried out. The terms bullying and mobbing are often used interchangeably in the European research, while American researchers tend to use the term counterproductive workplace behaviour, emotional abuse, workplace incivility, as well as the term bullying. Australian and New Zealand researchers tend to use the terms bullying and harassment.

Another reason why the meaning of the word 'bullying' can be unclear is that there are a number of different definitions of 'bullying'. The number of different terms used to describe bullying, and the different ways the phenomena is measured, results in different prevalence rates and outcomes in different studies. It also contributes to the confusion about what actually constitutes true workplace bullying. However, the following detailed definition is used by a number of researchers:

Bullying at work means harassing, offending or socially excluding someone or negatively affecting someone's work. In order for the label of bullying or mobbing to be applied to a particular activity the bullying behaviour has to occur repeatedly and regularly (e.g., weekly) and over a period of time (e.g., about six months). Bullying is an escalating process in the course of which the person confronted ends up in an inferior position and becomes the target of systematic negative social acts. A conflict cannot be called bullying if the incident is an isolated event or if two parties of approximately equal strength are in conflict. (Einarsen, Hoel, Zapf, & Cooper, 2011, p. 22)[1]

This definition is useful when conducting research as it provides a common way in which researchers can communicate their findings, particularly with respect to the prevalence of bullying behaviour. Other features of this definition are also useful as it takes into account issues pertaining to repetition, power and duration. These features are important when differentiating bullying from other types of conflict or inappropriate workplace behaviour. Other aspects of the definition, however, are problematic for common use in organisations. The inclusion of arbitrary time frames (weekly over about six months) appears illogical, because someone may be subjected to unreasonable behaviours for less than six months, or less regularly than on a weekly basis but might still suffer negative consequences as a result of being exposed to unreasonable and threatening behaviours. The inclusion of terms that require additional clarification (e.g., 'harassing', 'systemic acts') means that this description of bullying makes it difficult for employers and employees to understand what it is. The definition also fails to acknowledge the potential deleterious effects of bullying behaviours.

On the other end of the scale, many common definitions and ways of measuring bullying are too simplistic and some surveys or questionnaires about bullying even fail to provide a comprehensive definition, instead simply asking participants:

Have you been bullied at work? This can lead to a number of different behaviours inferred as bullying, and false positive bullying claims and statistics being cited.

As illustrated in the short quiz below, there is a possibility of four different answers, depending on how the question is asked; in other words, different results can be obtained depending upon how the term 'bullying' is defined.

The definition that I will be using throughout this book incorporates the main elements of the longer research definition above. However, it does not specify a time frame, and it reflects that bullying is essentially an OH&S hazard. Although there is no *one* legal definition of bullying in Australia, the definition below takes into account the important aspects of bullying, such as unreasonable behaviours, repeated behaviour, and the potential hazardous nature of the behaviour:

> Bullying is repeated hostile, or unreasonable behaviours targeting one or more employees, that a reasonable person, having taken into account all the relevant circumstances, would expect to cause harm the targets health.

Try the following short quiz.

BULLYING QUIZ

1. Have you been bullied at work?
2. Have you been bullied at work in the last 6 months?
3. Have you ever been the target of repeated hostile or unreasonable behaviours at work that either have made you ill or have had the potential to make you ill?
4. Have you been the target of repeated hostile or unreasonable behaviours at work in the last six months that either have made you ill, or have had the potential to make you ill?

Repeated

'Repeated' refers to the persistent and ongoing nature of the behaviours. The bullying might involve one specific behaviour repeated a number of times (i.e., yelling at a person repeatedly over time), or a number of different behaviours (i.e., yelling, giving someone the most unfavourable roster, and playing horrible, unwanted practical jokes). The repeated nature of the unreasonable behaviours means that the bullying occurs over a long period. Bullying is not an 'all or nothing' occurrence but s usually a process of worsening behaviours where targets over time are unable to defend themselves. Bullying often begins with low-grade bad behaviours or conflicts and ends with stigmatisation and active destruction of the target.[2]

Hostile or Unreasonable Behaviours

'Hostile, or unreasonable behaviours' refer to behaviours that a fair and sensible person who takes into account all the circumstances would see as victimising, humiliating, undermining or threatening. For example, most sensible people would see that repeatedly yelling at someone, giving them unfair or family unfriendly shifts all the time to punish them, or sending someone rude and humiliating emails is not a reasonable or acceptable standard of behaviour.

Bullying behaviours can include (but are not limited to):

- Verbal attacks such as yelling, name calling, continual put-downs, insulting behaviours and spreading malicious rumours or gossip.
- Unwelcome practical jokes, excessive sarcasm or teasing.
- Excluding behaviours such as stigmatisation, excluding someone from meetings or work functions for no good reason and freezing someone out of conversations or the workgroup.

- Denial or blocking of access to relevant information in order to cause harm to someone.
- Behaviours that specifically aim to undermine someone's performance.
- Inappropriate and intimidating text messages, emails or Facebook posts (commonly known as cyberbullying).
- Unreasonable exposure to an unmanageable workload over time for no justifiable reason.
- Continually singling out someone for the most unpopular or inconvenient shifts/tasks, or denying overtime.

Bullying and Power

Bullying involves a power imbalance. This means that the perpetrator uses their authority, power or influence in a way that undermines the other person, or people. In a normal conflict, two parties can have an argument or disagreement but do not necessarily inflict harm on each other. In bullying, the more powerful individual uses their power or influence to subjugate the other person. This power does not have to be hierarchical. We know that employees can bully their manager. Power and influence comes in many forms. A sole woman working in a male-dominated environment may have less influence or power than the men she is working with. A gay, lesbian, transgender or intersex employee will be more vulnerable to bullying than the dominant heterosexual group of employees they are working with. The employee with ten years or more of tenure and corporate knowledge may hold more authority with their peers than the new manager, worker or apprentice. The employee who appears confident and strong willed may hold more power than the shy employee. Employees who are in a vulnerable position are those who are likely to be marginalised because of a personal attribute that makes them susceptible.

Intention

There is significant debate as to whether the bullying behaviour needs to be intentional to be labelled bullying. Early research describes bullying as an intention or a perceived intention to harm. Early studies claimed that bullying was the result of a tyrannical personality where intent is inherent in the personality of the perpetrator.[3] However, we know that while some bullying can be intentional—for example, in predatory bullying where the perpetrator specifically targets someone with the purpose to oust them from the organisation or 'teach them a lesson'. However, not all bullying is

IF YOU THINK YOU ARE BEING BULLIED:

- Read the bullying policies and procedure in your organisation. What do they suggest?
- Find a respected manager to talk to.
- Talk to colleagues, family or friends about what is happening to you.
- Talk to your local doctor or psychologist, or your organisation's employee assistance provider (EAP).
- Talk to your trade union, Working Women's Centre[4] or OH&S authority.
- Do not retaliate or behave badly yourself. This will only provide ammunition to the person bullying you to justify their behaviour.
- Keep a record of what is happening, in case the problem escalates and you need to submit a formal complaint in the future.

IF YOU WITNESS BULLYING:

- Do not be a silent witness.
- Talk to a senior manager whom you trust. Managers have a legal obligation to prevent psychological hazards from occurring. They must intervene in some way.
- If it is safe and you feel confident, speak to the person who is behaving badly and let them know that their behaviour could be damaging to the target.
- Offer support to the target and help them find someone who may be able to assist them.

intentional. Some people may not realise that their behaviour is threatening or a risk to the other persons health and safety. However, even if it does not begin as intentional, as the behaviour escalates, a perpetrator's intention can emerge, as the more powerful person attempts to 'get rid of' the weaker. Despite this, most definitions of bullying do not include intent as a requirement because of the difficulty in observing this motivation. Just as laws relating to sexual harassment do not include intent as a criterion, intention is not a criterion of bullying.

Categories of Bullying

Bullying as Conflict Escalation

A lot of bullying begins with a conflict. It may be a conflict over values, needs or a specific way of doing things at work, or it may be labelled a 'personality clash'. It may be an interpersonal conflict. As illustrated in Figure 2.1, during the early stages, one of the parties might try to resolve the conflict in a constructive manner. However, often this is unsuccessful. As the conflict

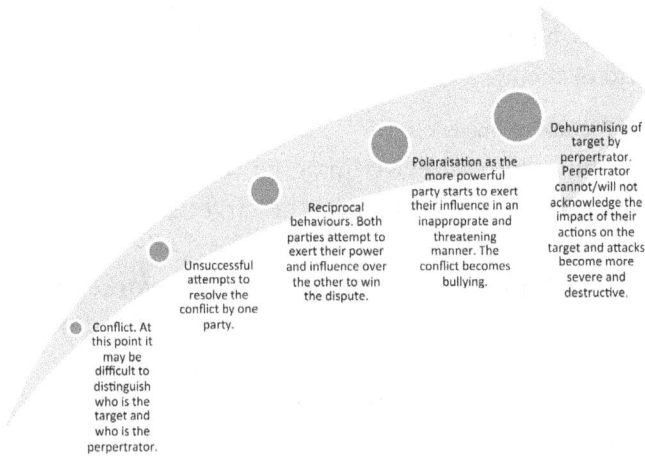

Figure 2.1
Development of conflict into bullying.

escalates, both parties become angry and defensive and often both may behave badly.

The norm of reciprocity suggests that we treat others how they treat us. So, if someone at work ignores us, it is likely we will ignore them back. If they are nasty to us, it is rare that we will be welcoming and friendly towards them, especially if we have tried to resolve the conflict with no success. This reciprocity of hostility can contribute to the conflict escalating further, polarising the relationship between the two parties into a target and perpetrator. Because of the power issues involved in bullying, as the behaviour becomes worse, one party is placed in a less powerful position, and the other uses their power or influence to oppress the target. According to some researches, workplace bullying is a particularly escalated form of conflict[4] where over time, the behaviour of the perpetrator becomes more extreme, as they aim to control the target. At the extreme end of the bullying spectrum, the perpetrator does not acknowledge the target as having feelings or emotion but is focused on 'getting rid of them'.

Bullying as Predatory Behaviour

Predatory bullying still exists in some workplaces. It begins with little or no provocation, and the target is the 'accidental victim'.

Predatory bullying often occurs when a worker from a marginalised group challenges the status-quo of a dominant in-group. The target is in a vulnerable position, and defence-less against the more powerful individuals within the group, and the group itself. Examples include a woman working in a traditionally male-dominated industry, a new migrant who has English as their second language working in a team of fluent English speaking Australians or a disabled worker working among able-bodied peers who do not believe they need to accommodate the disability of their colleague. In predatory bullying, the perpetrator/s are acting out their prej-

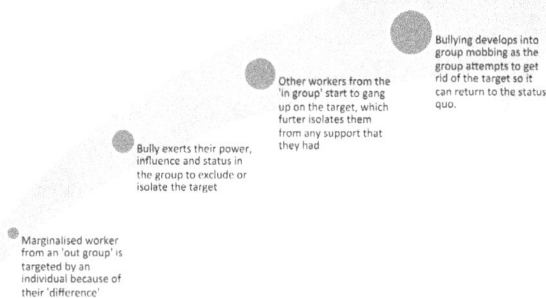

Bullying develops into group mobbing as the group attempts to get rid of the target so it can return to the status quo.

Other workers from the 'in group' start to gang up on the target, which furter isolates them from any support that they had

Bully exerts their power, influence and status in the group to exclude or isolate the target

Marginalised worker from an 'out group' is targeted by an individual because of their 'difference'

Figure 2.2
Predatory bullying can develop into group mobbing.

udice by targeting a vulnerable employee with the objective of removing them from the group so that the dominant culture can persevere. Predatory bullying often starts with one individual from the dominant group picking on the target and subjecting them to unreasonable behaviours. The individual usually holds significant power within the group and if their behaviour is not addressed, others from the dominant group start to support the 'bully'. Group bullying can occur as the group tries to expel the vulnerable individual. Group bullying is also known as mobbing.

Anti-discrimination and sexual harassment laws aim to provide protection for many types of bullying behaviours that target specific characteristics of a target. These laws aim to protect marginalised workers whose attributes are covered by this legislation. For example, age, race, sex, sexuality, disability to name a few. However, there are also many attributes that are not covered by anti-discrimination laws, and a target of predatory bullying may not necessarily be covered by the anti-discrimination legislation.

Aggression Framed as 'Normal' Behaviour

In some organisations, aggression is viewed as a legitimate managerial style. In these situations, staff are subjected to constant, intense pressure to perform and to reach very high targets or tight deadlines. The competitive and highly stressful nature of some businesses contributes to unreasonable management practices being normalised as 'the way we do things around here'. This approach means that unreasonable demands and management behaviours are ignored, and staff are implicitly encouraged not to talk about the stress that they are under or to identify the 'way of doing things' as bullying. In such cut-throat environments, employees who meet deadlines and achieve targets are rewarded, and they often start using their own power to overpower other staff who may threaten their own survival.

Often these industries or organisations are exemplified by high staff turnover, as employees who are unable to endure the stressful and aggressive culture leave.

Another approach that goes hand in hand with normalising bullying is one where organisations might have policies and complaints procedures that emphasise dignity and respect, but they treat complaints as personality clashes, or performance management issues. Therefore, they straight away treat the complainant as the problem rather than examining the alleged perpetrator's behaviour. They also fail to examine the wider organisational culture or risk factors that may have contributed to the alleged bullying. These approaches contribute to bullying behaviours accepted as part of the work culture without challenge.

In some organisations, blatant workplace bullying appears to be incorporated as part of the culture. Television programs such as *Ramsey's Kitchen* and *The Apprentice* glamorise humiliating behaviour and abuse as a necessary part of the job/industry to toughen up new workers and separate the weak from the strong. Wendy Bloisi and Helge Hoel, who wrote about bullying in commercial kitchens, reported that in many kitchens 'giving and receiving abuse is part of the socialisation process that creates the "hardness" needed to function in the commercial kitchen'.[5] Unfortunately, as illustrated by Stuart's case-study in chapter one, the behaviour that Stuart was subjected to as an apprentice chef in a commercial kitchen had dire consequences.

The Difference Between Bullying, Discrimination and Sexual Harassment

There is an overlap between what we know as bullying, sexual harassment and unlawful discrimination. All three can involve repeated inappropriate behaviours. While discrimination and sexual harassment are not traditionally looked at from within an OH&S framework, they too can contribute to employees suffering health problems and injury, especially if the discriminatory and harassing behaviours are repeated. However, unlike bullying, which involves repeated unreasonable behaviours; sexual harassment and unlawful discrimination, only require a single act to be unlawful.

Unlawful Discrimination

Discrimination is unfair or unequal treatment based on a person's specific attributes or characteristics. Anti-discrimination laws protect employees with specific attributes such as sex, sexuality, age, race, disability, marital status and so on. Unlike bullying, which involves repeated behaviour, treating an employee or customer unfavourably at work — even once — because of attributes covered by the anti-discrimination legislation may be unlawful. For example, refusing to promote an employee because he is too old, is age discrimination. Likewise, making disparaging remarks about an employee's race or ethnicity, is race discrimination.

Discrimination may be 'direct' or indirect. Direct discrimination is usually based on misinformation, prejudice and stereotypes, and is the most obvious form of discrimination. Some examples of direct discrimination and accompanying stereotypes:

- You cannot teach old dogs new tricks, so we will not hire anyone over 50. This is age discrimination.
- All men are aggressive, and we cannot have a man working in the child care centre. This is sex discrimination.
- The blokes will never accept a female boss, so we will not promote Kylie. This is sex discrimination.
- This applicant identifies as Aboriginal, so he will not be staying long. We better not offer him the job. This is race discrimination.
- Despite being the favoured applicant John had a past WorkCover injury (This past injury was not related to his current capacity to carry out this new job). However, John was

not offered the position because of his previous WorkCover claim. This is disability discrimination.

Indirect discrimination is not as obvious as direct discrimination. Indirect discrimination occurs when an organisation has a policy, requirement or a way of doing things that appears fair, but which has the effect of disadvantaging a certain group of people. However, when examined closely, the requirement itself is not reasonable. For example, in the past the police had a height requirement for all new applicants. However, this requirement disadvantaged female applicants. Because of the unreasonable nature of this requirement, it was changed. However, flight attendants are still required to be a certain height before they are accepted into training. This requirement is lawful and quite reasonable. Flight attendants need to be tall enough to open overhead lockers safely.

Other examples of indirect discrimination:

- A requirement that all applicants hold a current divers licence. If driving a vehicle is not part of the applicant's job, this could be indirect disability discrimination. However, if driving is an important part of their job, then this requirement is quite reasonable.

- A requirement that all managers be employed full-time. This may disadvantage those managers who wish to work part time after returning from maternity leave, and it may not be reasonable that part-time work or job sharing arrangements cannot be accommodated.

- A policy that all applicants for management positions must have five years continuous full-time management experience. This may indirectly discriminate against young applicants (age discrimination) who have the qualification for the position, but lack the experience, and women who have not had continuous service because of taking time out from their position to have a child (sex discrimination). When examined closely, the requirement might not be reasonable.

Indirect discrimination can also be ingrained in the 'culture' of an organisation as 'the way we do things around here'. For example — early morning meetings, 'golf' days and training weekends. These activities could potentially exclude certain groups of people, and be indirectly discriminating against them.

Sexual Harassment

Sexual harassment is often linked to bullying because frequently perpetrators incorporate sexually inappropriate comments and gestures into the range of bullying behaviours directed at a target. Sexual harassment can also occur on its own without being part of a pattern of bullying. Sexual harassment is covered by the federal sex discrimination legislation, and state anti-discrimination/equal opportunity legislation. The specific definitions of sexual harassment differ between these different pieces of legislation. However, generally sexual harassment refers to:

> any unwanted or unwelcome sexual behaviour, which makes a person feel offended, humiliated or intimidated.

The Australian Human Rights Commission (ARC) reports that:[6]

• Around one in three women in Australia aged 18 to 64 have experienced sexual harassment during their lifetime;

• The majority of sexual harassment is experienced in the workplace ;

• Over one in ten Australians have witnessed sexual harassment at work over the previous five years;

• Women are more likely to be targets of sexual harassment compared to men.

The most common types of reported sexually harassing behaviours include:

• unwelcome sexually suggestive comments or jokes that made the target feel offended

• physical intimidation, including unwelcome touching, hugging, cornering or kissing, inappropriate physical contact, or actual or attempted rape or assault

> ### SEXUAL HARASSMENT IS *NOT*
>
> ▨ mutual attraction
> ▨ reciprocated and shared acts of friendship
> ▨ respectful behaviour.

• sexually explicit emails or SMS messages.

Unlike bullying (which involves repeated acts), sexual harassment can result from a single incident. For example, touching somebody the breast on one occasion, or showing pornography to a workmate on one occasion can be sexual harassment if the behaviour is unwelcomed or offensive. As illustrated in the two case studies at the beginning of this book (Mick's story and Stuart's story), bullying, discrimination and sexually harassing behaviours can occur concurrently.

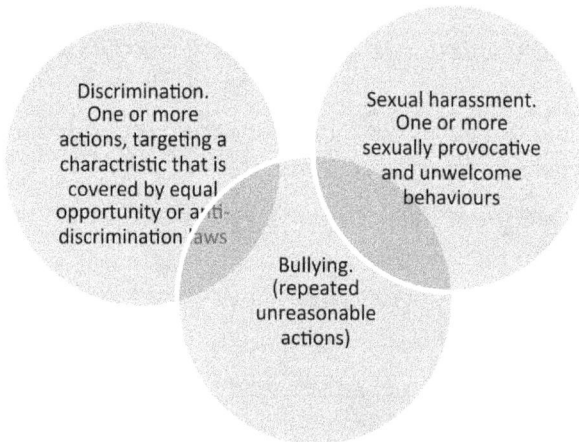

Discrimination.
One or more
actions, targeting a
charactristic that is
covered by equal
opportunity or anti-
discrimination laws

Sexual harassment.
One or more
sexually provocative
and unwelcome
behaviours

Bullying.
(repeated
unreasonable
actions)

Figure 2.3
The relationship between bullying, discrimination and sexual harassment.

Just as sexual harassment and bullying can co-occur, discrimination and bullying can also co-occur. In Debbie's story, Debbie was bullied by her co-workers who singled her out, bitched about her and refused to assist her in relation her visual impairment. As well as being repeated unreasonable behaviours (i.e. bullying), the behaviour that she describes, also fits the definition of disability discrimination.

Debbie's story: An example of bullying and disability discrimination combined

There were things like the dog; some of the other staff would say the dog was a hindrance because if she was sitting next to me, it might hinder them from getting from one post to the other faster. They were bitching and gossiping about me all the time and then not talking to me at all. There were also things around the computer. I was sharing with four people and they just refused to do anything that accommodated my disability around the software that I had to use … So I tried to negotiate things … but that didn't work. The more I tried, the more aggravation it caused because people felt that they had to be put out … Basically they didn't want me there. If I went to my team leader she would say things like why should you get special treatment, other people have rights too … It was such a degrading experience: It was like I couldn't read or write … It kept getting worse and worse to the stage that I was crying. I felt really out of control. I said that I had to leave. I have never been in a group of people that bitched about someone like that before — about me as a person, like I wasn't worth anything …

Mobbing

The term 'mobbing' is often used in the European bullying literature. Mobbing generally refers to a group of people bullying an individual. It most often occurs when a target has violated group norms, and the main objective of the mobbing behaviour is to banish the individual and remove them from the workplace.

Mobbing can be a form of group predatory bullying, or it can occur when a group turn on a whistle-blower and punish them for their behaviour, as illustrated below in Erin's story.

Erin's story: An example of mobbing

> I supposed I could be termed as a whistle-blower. I had spoken to management about practices that were happening where I was working that I didn't think were legal, that were definitely against the Code of Conduct … I know what I did was right and I don't think I could still be in that workplace watching what was going on, knowing what was going on and sit down and do nothing about it. It is a blatant misuse of finances and funds for someone to hire a car and charge it up to their manager and drive around in cars and order champagne — it just wasn't right … That's when the repercussions started to occur …

> I can't begin to tell you the effect that it had on me as a person. I ended up at (name of psychiatric hospital) for six weeks in hospital. I would sit and cry and eat and watch TV, probably 24 hours a day. I was very distrustful of people. I got to the stage where I didn't want to see anyone, didn't want to talk to anyone, didn't even want to go out to my letter box. Before I actually went on sick leave, I found what I was doing was leaving work, going to the pokies on the way home and spending so much money on the pokies because the way I was feeling was that I was a loser. People would go to the pokies knowing that they are not going to win, so what I was doing was just reinforcing that feeling. You're a loser, you are going to lose. I don't think I know that I am out of that deep dark hole yet. I still go to a hospital for treatment once a week. I still am very depressed. I lost my job, my friends I had there …

Erin's story also illustrates quite clearly the significant health effects of workplace bullying and mobbing.

Cyberbullying and Sexual Harassment

Information and communications technology (ICT) modalities are now an essential part of our daily lives, and in this new age of globalisation and rapidly advancing technology, the divide between work and home is becoming more blurred. The growth in electronic communication and social media is nothing short of astounding, and we cannot do without it. Most homes in Australia have a computer, and most of us have mobile phones, with smart phone technology fast taking over land lines and stand-alone cameras as the most popular way of keeping in touch. Consequently, cyberbullying and sexual harassment via the use of ICT is becoming more common. Many types of bullying and harassing behaviours that were once exclusively carried out face to face, are now also being carried out via modern technologies such as text messaging (through sending insulting texts or excluding a target in a text-message loop). Other types of bullying have occurred through Facebook, where employees have posted inappropriate and hurtful comments about colleagues and the organisation in general.

Many organisations have developed Internet policies in relation to appropriate use of the Internet and email systems, but many have not developed policies about appropriate use of technologies such as mobile phones, Twitter and Facebook. While most of the focus of cyberbullying has been in the area of school bullying, these new means of bullying and harassment also occur in the workplace. In a recent Australian court case, Malgorzata Poniatowska was awarded significant compensation because of the impact of two colleagues sexually harassing her through information technology.[7] The court found that one perpetrator sent her a number of lurid emails and text messages. The court found that her employer did not take reasonable steps to prevent or manage the allegations of sexual harassment Ms Poniatowska complained about, and as such she sustained a psychological injury because of the treatment that she was subjected to.[8]

This increase in ICT has the potential to change the face of both sexual harassment and workplace bullying, which now includes the target pursued through technologies that bridge the home/work domain. Employers and managers need to keep abreast of these changes in technology, as they pose unique risks.

The Work/Social Divide

Meetings and work functions where out of hours social drinks or dinners are held, especially in venues where alcohol is served and socialising occurs, create a high risk for inappropriate behaviour. Employers need to ensure that employees are not exposed to behaviours that may place them at risk of psychological (and physical) harm. In a high-profile Australian case, a former employee of David Jones claimed that she had been sexually harassed by the then Chief Executive at two work functions that involved alcohol and socialising. The subsequent publicity, and finally out-of-court settlement cost the organisation not only an undisclosed sum of money but considerable negative publicity. Work Christmas parties, retirement functions and farewells are notorious for incidents of bad behaviours after a few drinks. Employers need to know that despite the festivities, they are still responsible for the physical and psychological safety of all workers during these work functions even when they are held after hours, outside the normal workplace.

What Is Not Bullying

Most of us have reflected on occasions that we could have behaved better, dealt with a situation more constructively or listened to someone without becoming defensive. If we are truthful with ourselves, we all have behaved unreasonably at one time or another during the course of our working lives. However, this does not mean we have bullied someone. Not all unreasonable behaviours or experiences are bullying, even if these experiences contribute to someone feeling upset and aggrieved. Bullying is not a one-off altercation or argument, no matter how aggrieved the parties feel. A single incident of disrespectful behaviour is not bullying. However, in saying that, a single incident of unreasonable behaviour that is hurtful or harmful may escalate into bullying if not addressed and monitored.

Bullying is not:

• Performance management carried out in a respectful manner;

• Justifiable criticism carried out in a sensitive and respectful manner;

• A reasonable decision not to provide a benefit or incentive in connection with someone's employment, if that decision is justified and the same standards are applied to all employees.

• Unpopular administrative decisions or actions that are justified under the circumstances.

• A management decision that employees don't necessarily agree with, is not workplace bullying.

Case study: Reasonable management action that is not bullying.

Mira works in the purchasing department of a large organisation; She has been there for six months and works with six other staff. The department is busy and the work required is routine and shared evenly among the seven workers.

On a regular basis Mira falls behind schedule with her tasks, and appears to be struggling with her duties. Mira's manager holds a private meeting with her in order to discuss the difficulties she is having, and talk about how her performance can be improved. Mira is asked to attend a two day training course to help her develop more skills to assist her in carrying out her job. This course will be paid for by the workplace, and Mira will not lose any pay or entitlements by attending the course. Mira's manager has also agreed to provide Mira with extra time to complete her tasks for a specific time period while she is updating her skills. Mira feels humiliated and singled out, even though her manager has counselled her in regard to her underperformance with sensitively and respect. While Mira feels upset by what is occurring, she is not being bullied.

Bullying is not low-grade discourteous behaviour. Bullying is serious, and involves repeated threatening behaviours. Because of the ongoing nature and the seriousness the behaviours there is a risk to the health or safety of targets. Unless rude behaviour is part of a pattern of increasing threating and unreasonable behaviours, unprofessional or discourteous behaviours such as someone 'not saying good morning to you', or 'not inviting you to morning tea', in and of itself is not bullying. It may be rude, but on its own, it does not pose a risk to your health and safety. Likewise, managing someone's performance based on reasonable standards and carried out in a respectful manner is not bullying, even if the employee feels aggrieved by being counselled, or having their performance managed. Low-grade rude or unprofessional behaviours, and unresolved workplace conflicts may need addressing by a manager, as they have the potential to escalate into bullying if left unchecked. However, they are not necessarily bullying in and of themselves.

A physical altercation or physical fight is not bullying; it is assault. Violence is a risk to the safety of employees and should not be accepted in *any* form. Incidents of violence or assault should be referred to the police.

Managers are allowed to guide, warn and counsel their employees, critique their work and performance, and discipline them if it is reasonable to do so, and if they do it in a respectful way, according to organisational policy standards and guidelines. Managers sometimes make unpopular decisions, implement unpopular processes, deny requests and set performance goals, standards and deadlines. However, if this behaviour is legitimate and has a justifiable operational explanation, it is not bullying — even if it is unpopular. An employee who is not working to acceptable standards may require more supervision than other employees. This high level of supervision is not bullying, if it is justified and carried out respectfully. However, each employee must be subjected to the same standards. Requiring one employee to perform at a comparatively higher standard, may be bullying if it is unreasonable.

In a recent court case, the complainant, an employee who suffered with a physical disability, alleged that her manager and several other employees with whom she worked had bullied, harassed and discriminated against her. She alleged that instead of accommodating her disability and helping her, her manager singled her out by not promoting her, spoke to her in a physically intimidating manner, required her to carry out work below her qualifications and would not provide a workstation that would accommodate her physical needs.

However, in a 60,000-word judgement, Magistrate Brown found that the complainants allegations were unfounded. Instead, he found that *her own* behaviour towards her manager and co-workers at times may have constituted bullying. He found that her manager had taken a number of reasonable steps to accommodate her disability and had hired a number of professionals to help her, including physiotherapists, ergonomic specialists, occupational physicians and OH&S specialists. However, despite her employer providing significant evidence as to how they had tried to help her adjust to the workplace, she would not carry out reasonable requests by her manager, and consistently questioned the motives and agenda of management. In his judgement, Magistrate Brown said:

> I am satisfied that the evidence indicates that, throughout her time as an APS2 officer, [the complainant] waged a passive campaign, based on intransigence and obstruction to management, to secure her preferred outcome ... which was to have a research

> position based at a higher [APS level] ... I have come to the conclusion that [the complainant] did indeed use her undoubted familiarity with the mechanisms of complaint as an instrument of intimidation against the respondent and its agents.

He went on to say that:

> At times, with the benefit of hindsight, it could be said that some of the Commonwealth's agents could have acted quicker or have communicated better or more empathetically with [the complainant] ... Individual members of the management team reacted to this tension from time to time, not always with composure. These reactions may be criticised for being unprofessional. However, in my view, they do not amount to harassment for the purposes of the applicable legislation.[9]

This case highlights that reasonable management actions are not bullying. While employers need to accommodate an employee's disability, they have the right to counsel, instruct, refuse to promote and warn employees about the consequences of poor behaviours if these warnings are justified. Employees who challenge appropriate and lawful directions, and intimidate managers and fellow employees through verbal threats, serial complaints and harassment may in fact be carrying out behaviours themselves that amount to bullying.

Who Bullies Whom?

Bullying can occur between staff (horizontal bullying), by managers towards their staff (downwards bullying) and by workers towards their managers (upwards bullying). While traditionally most of the bullying research has found that managers are the more likely to be the perpetrators, managers who are subjected to bad behaviour by their staff may be less likely to report that they are being bullied because they feel that it is part of their job to manage poor behaviours. Some managers believe that if they complain about a staff member's behaviour and admit that they find the behaviour intimidating, they will be labelled as incompetent or weak. New managers and supervisors especially need

WORKPLACE BULLYING IS *NOT*

- Reasonable directions and instructions based on operational requirements.

- Performance management, critique or criticism about an employee's work that is justified.

- Decisions not to provide promotion, training or any other benefits, based on reasonable standards and justifiable operational circumstances.

- A physical altercation or physical violence is assault and not bullying (although it may be part of a pattern of bullying). This behaviour should be reported to the police.

- A one-off conflict or argument with a manager or co-worker is not bullying, but may need to be addressed.

- A single incident of bad behaviour is not bullying, but also may need to be addressed.

- Low-grade annoying or unprofessional behaviours and conflict that may be annoying, but do not affect the targets health or safety, are not bullying. However, if not addressed, they could escalate into bullying.

support and mentoring in how to manage their staff respectfully, and how to manage poor performance and bad behaviours in their workgroup. Sometimes junior or less experienced managers can react to employees behaving badly by behaving badly themselves and using their managerial power in a way that can become bullying if not addressed. They need assistance and mentoring from more experienced managers and need to learn how to respectfully manage employees who are behaving in a threatening or aggressive manner toward them. Managers need to learn how to respond to bad behaviours rather than react. Senior managers play a vital role in setting the standards of behaviour they want the organisation to follow. Senior managers who bully staff and treat others in a disrespectful manner contribute to junior managers following their bad example.

Sarah's story: An example of upwards bullying

> I was trying to manage him but his behaviour got worse and worse and I went to my own manager for support and I said I have tried this, this and this, and I have tried a lot of techniques to defuse his behaviour … but if I said anything that he interpreted as negative, he would lose the plot. Yell, rant, rave, tell me I didn't know anything. Huff and puff, basically, made derogatory belittling comments to me (participant crying). Sorry, it still gets me emotional. In effect, he was bullying me. He would try to intimidate me to do things his way. It was really bizarre. It was escalating to the point that he would throw a tantrum: in the door to my office, he would stand up, stomp around, lean across my desk at me, just about spitting in my face and then go storming out down the corridor flinging comments back.

What Laws Apply

The acceptability of bullying in the workplace has changed considerably over the last 20 years or so. Behaviours that were once considered 'robust' supervision, customary initiation practices or personality conflicts, are now recognised as hazardous, and if not bullying in themselves, are an occupational health and safety risk. Depending on the circumstances and the behaviours, targets of workplace bullying, sexual harassment and unlawful discrimination can rely on a number of pieces of legislation to address the problem. Penalties may apply when regulatory bodies such as OH&S agencies take employers to court for failing to provide a safe system of work and prevent or appropriately manage workplace bullying or other hazards that have contributed to a worker being injured.

In Australia, there is no one law that covers bullying, sexual harassment and discrimination. Instead, a number of different pieces of State and Federal legislation cover these separate, but overlapping constructs. Sexual harassment and discrimination are covered by the anti-discrimination or equal opportunity legalisation in Australia. Workplace bullying is covered by the OH&S legislation. This can be confusing for targets because they have to decide whether the behaviour they have been subjected to is bullying, discrimination or sexual harassment. Often the behaviour is a mixture of all three, but the legal avenues available are vastly different if the behaviour is sexual harassment or discrimination as opposed to bullying.

Employees who believe they are being sexually harassed or discriminated against can lodge a complaint with the relevant anti-discrimination or equal opportunity authority. To have recourse under the anti-discrimination or equal opportunity legislation a target must show that they have been bullied *because* of a particular attribute that is covered by those laws for example, their age, sex, disability, age, and so on.

Complaints under the anti-discrimination or equal opportunity legislation need to be made through the Federal Human Rights Commission or though the complainants State equal opportunity or anti-discrimination commission. Complaints that meet the criteria usually proceed through a process of conciliation. Conciliation is a confidential process and is a form of mediation, where all the parties come together with the aim or resolving the dispute. Conciliation has been described as:

> a process in which the participants to a dispute, with the assistance of a third person (the conciliator), identify the issues in dispute, develop options, consider alternatives and endeavour to reach an agreement. The conciliator has an advisory role, but not a determinative one. The conciliator may suggest and/or give expert advice on possible options

for resolving the issues in dispute and may actively encourage the participants to reach an agreement. In conciliation processes the parties are often accompanied by expert advisers, including legal advisers.[10]

Most complaints of discrimination or sexual harassment are resolved at a conciliation conference and do not proceed to court. If the conciliation is unsuccessful, either the Commissioner will decide to terminate the complaint, or if it appears to have substance, will send it to court to have the matter resolved. (If the commissioner decides to terminate the case, the complainant can still apply to the court to have the matter heard.) However, there are often lengthy delays in the process, and complaints can take years from the lodgement of the complaint, to get to court. If the complainant takes a complaint to court themselves, and is unsuccessful, they may be also responsible for their own and the responders legal costs. Taking a complaint through this process can be very daunting, especially for a complainant who is suffering an injury because of the alleged behaviour.

The recent harmonisation of the Australian occupational health and safety laws highlight the responsibilities that a person conducting a business or undertaking has in ensuring that employees are not exposed to health and safety risks including psychological hazards such as bullying.

A number of state occupational health and safety regulatory authorities have developed guidance material and codes of practice that provide information for employers on how to prevent and manage bullying from an OH&S perspective. These include WorkSafe Victoria 2009,[11] Workplace Health and Safety Queensland 2004,[12] WorkSafe Western Australia, 2006,[13] and SafeWork SA, 2005.[14] These guides are useful resources for organisations that seek to prevent and manage bullying from within this OH&S framework.

Some targets of bullying can utilise the industrial relations laws if they have been unfairly dismissed or have had had no choice but to leave their employment as a result of workplace bullying. However employees wanting to use this legislation may be limited by certain exclusion criteria including employees earning above a specific threshold, probationary employees, and casual employees who are not covered by an award or enterprise agreement.[15]

Workers who believe they have been unfairly dismissed because of bullying should seek legal or industrial advice in order to determine whether they are eligible to address their dismissal through the industrial court.

If a target is assaulted because of bullying, or is sexually assaulted (an extreme form of sexual harassment) they should notify the police. Serious bullying is now part of the Victorian Crimes Act. The *Crimes Amendment (Bullying) Bill 2011* made the offence of stalking apply to situations of serious bullying. It broadens the 'course of conduct' carried out by the perpetrator to include behaviour such as making threats to the target and acting in ways that could reasonably be expected to cause the target to engage in self-harm. These amendments to the Crimes Act were a response to a Victorian case which resulted in an young waitress committing suicide after being subjected to serious bullying in the workplace. Unfortunately, these laws of little to prevent the behaviour in the first place, instead focusing on the perpetrators behaviour after the bullying has escalated to a dangerous level.

In a recent review of bullying and harassment legal cases that have proceeded through the Australian legal system, Patricia Easteal and Josie Hampton found that complaints were more likely to be upheld when complainants went through the OH&S or the industrial relations pathways, as opposed to using the anti-discrimination legislation. However, they found that most bullying (including discrimination and harassment) complaints were settled informally outside of court, and more than half of the bullying and harassment complaints that went to court were not successful. These results highlight that while there are a number of legal options available to targets of bullying and harassment, each has its limitations, and there is no overall remedy for bullying per se.[16]

Why People Do Not Complain

As the previous section highlighted, there are a number of laws that protect people from workplace bullying, sexual harassment and discrimination; however, they can be tricky to navigate, and not many complaints end up in court, let alone are successful.

While the media often highlight the number of unsubstantiated bullying complaints received by regulatory authorities, what they fail to highlight is that many targets of bullying and harassment have significant difficulties making complaints. Often the background variables that allow bad behaviours to develop and escalate are the same factors that prevent a target from speaking out, and complaining internally.

Some of the reasons why targets do not complain include:

- If a target's manager has a style that has effectively ignored bad behaviour (laissez faire management style), or has contributed to it (authoritarian management style), it will make it very difficult for a target to speak out against the behaviour.

- If a target's manager is participating in inappropriate behaviours themselves, it is very difficult for a target to complain.

- If a target is part of a marginalised group and trying to fit in, they will be less likely to complain about the behaviour of the group and may even participate in inappropriate behaviours themselves in order to be part of the group.

- A target of bullying or harassment might be too scared to report the behaviour in case they are threatened further or victimised for speaking out.

- Workers who are most vulnerable to being bullied or harassed are those without power. This sense of powerlessness is made worse by the bullying behaviours that they are exposed to. Bullied employees who have a psychological injury such as depression or anxiety will have poor confidence, low self-esteem and may not be in a position to stand up for themselves and complain.

- Workers from non-English speaking countries, ad different cultures may not be aware of their rights in Australia, and may not be aware that they can complain about unreasonable, harassing or discriminating behaviours that they are subjected to in the workplace.

- There may be no avenues for complaint. Respectful behaviour policies may not be easily accessible.

- Bullies can be very powerful people in senior positions. If a manager is being bullied by the chief executive officer (CEO), head of HR or another person in an executive position, it is very difficult for them to complain. Complaining about a senior or high profile person in the organisation might be seen as a 'career limiting move' and the target viewed as a troublemaker.

- Managers often do not complain about being bullied by their staff as they see that it is part of their job to manage poor behaviours. Because of this, upwards bullying, or managers being bullied by subordinates may be an underreported phenomena.

- Targets of workplace bullying may not complain because they have seen issues brushed under the carpet when people have complained in the past. They therefore think there is no point in complaining.

- Many bullying behaviours are covert and are such difficult to prove. Targets might have a difficult time proving they are being bullied, especially if the workplace environment accepts bullying behaviour as normal.

Endnotes

1 Einarsen, S., Hoel, H., Zapf, D., & Cooper, C. (2011). The concept of bullying and harassment at work: The European tradition. In S. Einarsen, H. Hoel, D. Zapf & C. Cooper (Eds.), *Bullying and harassment in the workplace: Developments in theory, research and practice* (2nd ed., pp. 3–32). London, England: CRC Press.

2 Zapf, D., & Gross, C. (2001). Conflict escalation and coping with workplace bullying: A replication and extension. *European Journal of Work and Organisational Psychology, 10*(4), 497–522.

3 Ashforth, B. (1994). Petty tyranny in organisations. *Human Relations, 47,* 755–778.

4 Zapf, D. & Gross, C. (2001). Conflict escalation and coping with workplace bullying. A replication and extension. *European Journal of Work and Organisational Psychology, 10,* 497–522.

5 Bloisi, W., & Hoel, H. (2008). Abusive work practices and bullying in commercial chefs. *International Journal of Hospitality Management, 27,* 649–656.

6 AHRC. (2008). Sexual harassment: A serious business. *Results of the 2008 Sexual Harassment National Telephone Survey.* Retrieved from www.hreoc.gov.au/sexualharassment/serious_business/SHSB_Report2008.pdf

7 *Poniatowska v Hickinbotham* [2009] FCA 680

8 *Poniatowska v Hickinbotham* [2009] FCA 680

9 *Sluggett v Commonwealth of Australia* [2011] FMCA 609

10 National Alternative Dispute Resolution Advisory Council. *What is ADR: Conciliation.* Retrieved from http://www.nadrac.gov.au/www/nadrac/nadrac.nsf/Page/What_is_ADRConciliation

11 WorkSafe Victoria. (2009). *Preventing and responding to bullying at work* (3rd ed.). Melbourne, Australia: WorkSafe Victoria and WorkCover NSW.

12 Workplace Health and Safety Queensland. (2004). *Prevention of workplace harassment code of practice.* Brisbane, Australia: Author.

13 WorkSafe Western Australia. (2006). *Code of practice: Violence, aggression and bullying at work.* Perth, Australia: Author.

14 SafeWork SA. (2005). *Preventing workplace bullying a practical guide for employers and employees.* Interagency Round Table on Workplace Bullying 2005, Adelaide, Australia.

15 *Fair Work Act 2009* (Cth)

16 Easteal, P., & Hampton, J. (2011). Who is the 'Good' bullying victim/corpse? *Canberra Law Review, 19*(2), 63–83.

Australian Legislation	Circumstances that may apply
Australian Federal anti discrimination and sexual harassment laws	These Federal anti-discrimination laws protect people from being subjected to unreasonable and unfair treatment at work because of specific personal attributes. These attributes are known as 'grounds', and complainants need to show that they have been treated unfavourably because of a specific 'ground', before they can make a compliant of discrimination.
State anti-discrimination and equal opportunity laws	Each State also has its own relevant equal opportunity or anti-discrimination laws that protect individuals at work from mistreatment because of specific 'grounds'.
Criminal laws	When bullying behaviour involves assault, stalking, theft, imprisonment or other types of criminal activity, then State or Federal criminal laws may apply, and the behaviour should be reported to the police.
Common law	Under common law, employers have a duty of care to protect their employees from workplace hazards, including behaviours that cause injury.
Occupational Health and Safety laws	These OH&S laws highlight that employers have a duty of care to provide a safe workplace for their employees. This duty of care extends to preventing physical and psychological hazards and injuries.
	Under these laws employers are obliged to take reasonable measures to prevent bullying. Failure to take 'reasonable measures' to prevent bullying can result in significant penalties for employers, and individual perpetrators if an injury occurs.
Enterprise agreements and other industrial instruments	Many awards and industrial agreements also contain sections that prohibit unlawful discrimination and bullying, and contain dispute resolution procedures for addressing grievances.
Codes of conduct and Respectful Behaviour Policies	As part of preventing bullying, organisations have policies or codes of conduct that all employees need to adhere to. Breaches can result in disciplinary action including dismissal.
Constructive dismissal aspects of industrial relations law	If the workplace bullying becomes so bad, that an employee is forced to leave for their own safety, they may be able to claim compensation for 'constructive dismissal' under industrial relations laws.

CHAPTER 3

The Impact of Workplace Bullying

The Health Effects of Bullying

There is a large body of research that reports the detrimental psychological and physical effects of workplace bullying, not only for targets but also for witnesses and bystanders. The workplace bullying literature consistently highlights the relationship between bullying and psychological stress reactions, insomnia, mental health problems and physical ill health.[1]

In an early study of the consequences of workplace bullying, it was reported that targets of bullying reported higher levels of anxiety, depression and psychosomatic complaints than nontargets.[2] A number of studies since then have supported this early finding and have shown that workplace bullying can have a harmful effect on a target's physical and mental health along a continuum from increased risk of cardiovascular disease to depression, anxiety and posttraumatic stress disorder. In extreme cases, the mental health problems caused by workplace bullying have also led to the target committing suicide. Anxious and depressed workers are more prone to making mistakes, performing badly in their job, being snappy and argumentative, withdrawing from their team and viewing their organisation through a negative lens. Targets of workplace bullying have also been found to take significantly more drugs than non-bullied workers.[3] One study found that around 4% of nonbullied workers took drugs. However, this changed to 20% of workers taking drugs to cope with work if they believed they were a victim of workplace bullying. These results suggest that taking illicit drugs or medication to cope with bullying can be a serious problem and illicit drug use can contribute to increased mental health problems, and also increased risk of accidents and physical injuries at work. Anecdotal evidence (see Stuart's story in chapter 1) suggests that when bullied targets take illicit drugs to cope with the behaviour they are being exposed to, their drug-taking behaviour can become the focus of the investigation rather than the behaviour of the bullying perpetrator.

Witnesses of workplace bullying have also been found to suffer poor mental health as a result of the environment in which they are working. Studies have found that employees who witnesses workplace bullying are more likely to leave the workplace than nonbullied employees,[4] and they also suffer greater levels of stress and anxiety than employees who do not witness bullying.[5]

Ike

> That weekend, I went home to bloody hang myself. I wrote a note, and if it wasn't for my daughter, I wouldn't me here now. I had a nice piece of white rope. I had it all tied up and ready to go. But my daughter, she knew something was wrong and rang up and came around.

Brenda

I have never felt that out of control before. I felt it was really unprofessional … I felt like I wanted to go and kill myself. So, I went home and I actually took 40 Panadeine Forte. Nothing happened actually, didn't die, obviously it wasn't enough, and the next day I went, I have a really good relationship with my doctor and told her what I had done.

Loralie

My self-esteem and confidence were seriously blocked. It was a very personal attack and … I found this damaged my capacity to feel confident and comfortable with other people because initially I wasn't sure how my behaviour was being interpreted. Also, I was very teary, very depressed, for quite some time and very highly sensitive in that regard. Somebody would look at me and I would burst into tears.

James

I just felt absolutely horrible. My head was going to burst. I felt sick in the stomach … I was very emotional, and I was very sick, and I thought I was going to have another heart attack. That's how bad I felt. I hardly slept … Whenever I went to the psychologist, I would break down and end up sick for days. I have never had that sort of reaction in my life and I have dealt with major disagreements, abusive customers and staff. That was one of my strengths.

Current research that I am undertaking highlights the serious long term repercussions of workplace bullying. The ongoing negative impact of bullying on the research participants highlights how bullying is an extreme stress and threat that has left many participants unable to function as they once did. All the research participants that I have been talking with are no longer able to work because of their injuries. All have severe clinical levels of Depression and Anxiety, most have symptoms of Post-Traumatic Stress Disorder. These injuries are compounded by them now being unemployed and facing significant barriers trying to get back into the workforce, while at the same time coping with the impact of the past bullying. Many talked with me about their fundamental belief of the world as a safe place being shattered by their experiences. Work was once a source of pride and provided a positive outlet for their skills and abilities. However, work is now seen as threatening, and scary. Because many past targets have become highly vigilant and anxious, neutral behaviours (such as someone from work ringing them to see how they are feeling), are now interpreted as threatening, and situations that are mildly threatening (such as applying for a job or meeting new people), cause high levels of fear and avoidance.

The recent Government enquiry into Workplace Bullying in Australia found that as well as the specific psychological injuries that were being reported by targets of bullying, there were physical reactions such as chest pain, stomach ulcers, hair loss, and irritable bowel syndrome. These psychological and physical injuries were contributing to social isolation, withdrawal from family and friends, loss of social outlets and ongoing unemployment.[6] Workplace bullying impacts not only targets, but siblings, children, partners, wives and husbands of targets.

Recent studies also suggest that being accused of bullying is a stressful experience and managers who are accused of bullying can also suffer from significant anxiety, depression and stress.[7]

Just because someone is a perpetrator, does not mean that they deserve to be bullied themselves. As a human beings, we all deserve to be treated with dignity and respect, just as we all need to be responsible for our actions. The following individual cases highlight that all people involved in a bullying investigation require support throughout the process, even those accused of being a bully.

Senior manager, private industry — accused of bullying

It affected me severely. I became suicidal. Seriously, I was devastated, mortified, and began to question what I had done and to whom … it was the worst period of my entire life. I suffered a racing heart — my blood pressure escalated; I experienced my first ever panic attack; I had a continual pressure in my chest; I could not eat; I felt I could trust no one; I became deeply depressed.

Team leader, private industry — accused of bullying

I had a lot of anxiety… It was like walking on eggshells and then the following week I just couldn't …. I had to control myself at work (participant crying). Even up to now … because of that incident when he said I was talking about someone, and he first accused me in August, and since then I'm not sleeping well. I would sleep till about two o'clock, three o'clock in the morning and … it takes a lot of energy to face the day and say you have to go to work, I was so anxious and had nowhere to turn…

Bullying and OH&S

Although OH&S laws were traditionally focused on physical hazards such as electrical safety, preventing falls, or managing dangerous chemicals, the negative health impact of bullying is becoming more apparent. This is partly because of the costs associated with psychological injury, which include the significant medical, legal, business and costs of compensation claims, and because of the increased publicity in relation to the adverse health consequences of bullying.

While work related 'mental disorder' claims have generally fallen over the last five years in Australia, this group of claimants consistently require the longest amount of time off work, with a cost of more than double that of physical injury claims.[8] The average mental disorders claim is around 10.8 weeks, and work related stress claims consistently have the longest time lost, almost three times more than the median time off work for other serious workers compensation claims of 4.0 weeks.[9]

The Australian courts have paid out significant compensation to claimants as a result of bullying sexual harassment and discrimination. Compensation is usually based on:

- legal costs
- medical and hospital costs
- economic loss (past earnings, and future earning capacity)
- compensation for psychological or physical injury, pain and suffering
- punitive damages (when an employer is held to be negligent).

A number of organisations have also been fined by regulatory bodies breaches of OH&S laws that have contributed to workplace bullying and psychological injury.

WorkSafe Victoria v Ballarat Radio Pty Ltd [10]

This was one of the first Australian cases where an organisation was convicted of workplace bullying independent of litigation by a target. WorkSafe Victoria, the Victorian OH&S regulatory authority took Ballarat Radio to court for breaches of the Victorian OH&S act after the investigation revealed that one of the announcers subjected employees to verbal abuse and threats of violence at work over a number of years. The Court heard that the radio station had allowed the announcer to verbally and physically abuse a number of staff until just before his sacking. The radio station had no complaint mechanisms, no training had taken place in regards to the rights and responsibilities of staff, and management failed to stop the bullying when they became aware of it. The organisation was convicted and fined $25,000 for failing to provide a safe workplace to its employees, and $25,000 for failing to provide instruction, training and supervision in relation to bullying. It was also ordered to pay costs of $5,000. The individual perpetrator was separately convicted and fined $10,000 and ordered to pay costs of $1700.

McKenna v Victoria Police[11]

This was a sexual harassment and discrimination claim where Ms Mckenna alleged that she had been discriminated against because of her marital status and sex. The tribunal found that Ms Mckenna's employer (the Victoria Police) and three colleagues were responsible for bullying her, and that she had also been sexually harassed. She was awarded $125,000 for hurt feelings, distress and psychological illness.

The Café Vamp Case[12]

A Melbourne cafe owner was convicted and fined under Victoria's *Health and Safety Act 2004* for failing to provide a safe work environment, after a waitress committed suicide following workplace bullying. The court was told that Brodie Panlock, aged 19, was bullied by three workmates while her employer allowed the behaviour to go on. The magistrate convicted and fined the four individual perpetrators as well as the director of the company that owned the café. A breakdown of the fines are as follows:

- Map Foundation Pty Ltd trading as Café Vamp: Convicted and fined $110,000.
- Director: Convicted and fined $30,000
- Individual perpetrator 'A': Convicted and fined $45,000
- Individual perpetrator 'B': Convicted and fined $30,000
- Individual perpetrator 'C': Convicted and fined $10,000.

Naidu v Group 4 Securitas Pty Ltd & Anor[13]

In one of the largest Australian payouts made in regard to workplace bullying, Mr Nadu was awarded nearly $2 million compensation after the court found that he had been subjected to serious repeated harassment, duress, racial and sexual abuse, humiliation, unreasonable workloads and pressure, and threats of violence and financial harm by another employee. As a result, of the bullying and harassment that he was subjected to, Mr Naidu suffered serious posttraumatic stress disorder and major depression. He was unable to work again. He was awarded $2 million damages, which included lost salary of $70,000 a year until the age of 65, general damages of $200,000 and exemplary damages against the employer of $150,000.

Nikolich v Goldman Sachs J B Were Services Pty Ltd[14]

Mr Nikolich, alleged that he was bullied by his employer and was subjected to a series of malicious personal attacks, verbal abuse and insults, and his clients had been reallocated to other colleagues. He said that despite making a formal complaint about the behaviour, nothing was done, and he eventually went on sick leave because of the impact of the behaviour. However, while on leave, his employment contract was terminated. In court Mr Nikolich successfully argued that his employer's failure to deal with his compliant was a breach of their own workplace bullying policies and complaint procedures. He said that the termination of his employment constituted a breach of his employment contract, and a breach of the Workplace Relations Act. The court found that there had been bullying, and that his employer had failed to comply with the organisations policy promising to 'take every practicable step' to protect the employees' 'health and safety'. Mr Nikolich was awarded around $500,000 in damages. The findings were appealed, but the Full Court of the Federal Court in upheld that decision.[15]

These cases highlight the potential costs to individual perpetrators, and responsible people within the organisation when bullying, sexual harassment and discrimination cases area substantiated by the courts. When examined from the human perspective, these cases are also a sobering reflection of the personal effects of psychological hazards in the workplace. They are a reminder that workplace bullying and harassment has a significant human cost when workers are injured by the hazardous nature of another person's behaviours.

Because of the psychological damage that bullying can engender to not only the target but others witnessing the behaviours, OH&S legislation in many countries including Australia now recognises bullying as a health-and-safety hazard. Therefore, all employers, company directors, managers, and employees have a specific legal responsibility to do everything that is reasonably practical to prevent bullying, sexual harassment and discrimination (the hazard) from occurring in their organisation and to take immediate action to stop it, if it does occur.

What About the Psychopaths?

Society's understanding of bullying and how to tackle it, is significantly influenced by the media. Books with emotive titles that include 'psychopath' or 'monster' are typically sensational, adversarial and dramatic. Some books and magazine articles go so far as to provide descriptions of psychopathic personality traits and diagnostic criteria so that readers can self-diagnose psychopaths at work. This approach merely stigmatises individuals without providing direction or assistance to organisations who want to prevent or stop bullying from occurring. Suggesting that psychopaths in the workplace are a common occurrence also encourages disgruntled employees to diagnose people at work, and encourages organisations to focus on individuals, rather than address inappropriate behaviours from an evidence based risk management approach. Lara Crawshaw[16] made the valid point that we don't see books on the shelves with titles such as 'Evil Parents and Their Prey' or 'Kiddy Kickers'. Instead, these issues are treated seriously (as they should be) and approached thoughtfully in the parenting and child abuse literature. Why is it then that much of the bullying literature is simplistic and sensational, and fails to offer well-considered solutions to address the problem?

While I was recruiting participants for a study that involved interviewing accused bullies, the following commentary was posted on a web site. It was written in red, some of it in bold and in capital letters. I felt intimidated, as I was warned not to carry out my research and to stay away from the 'psychopaths'.

But how will you differentiate between the decent managers who are trying to 'do the right thing' and the psychopaths, Moira?

Psychopaths are such good liars. And, in my own real-life experience — Psychopathic state school principals seem to enjoy the experience of bullying.

They enjoy 'spinning' reasons to punish a teacher. They enjoy asking senior officers for 'advice'. They enjoy gossiping about the person that they are planning to attack.

They enjoy manipulating senior officers, other principals and teachers and being the centre of attention.

And I strongly suspect that they will enjoy manipulating you, Moira. Psychopaths don't seem to know that they are psychopaths.

They never seem to develop any insight into their abuse.

Psychopaths never seem to experience any remorse for the effect of their bullying on the health and the career of their targets. And they never make any commitment to stop their workplace abuse.

They don't have to.

Bullying can be 'spun' into something with another name, Moira. 'All sorts of workplace conflict and behaviours that are not necessarily bullying' can be used to excuse bullying.

This seems to be a strategy. Look out for it, Moira. Don't let the psychopaths manipulate you, Moira or you and your research will become part of the problem …

I would suggest, Moira, we also need to know —

- the strategies that psychopathic managers use to 'get away with' workplace abuse.
- how they learned those strategies. Who teaches psychopathic managers how to 'get away with it'?

- and how bullying benefited the psychopaths — the applause, the celebrations in the Parliament House annex, the chocolate cakes, the promotions and the awards that the psychopaths have received as a result of their bullying.

- and how many employees the psychopaths have successfully managed to drive into ill health retirement/suicide/ out of work.

I think you've got it the wrong way round, Moira. First the bullying begins, and then the workplace conflict develops. Psychopaths seem to 'try out' a few different strategies until they find a strategy that will 'stick'. The psychopaths don't need any more support, Moira ....

The views expressed in the above commentary are very emotive and are not at all helpful. Instead, they promulgate the misperception that *all bullies* (or even those *accused* of being bullies) are psychopaths, and they fail to address the question as to what factors make a person behave badly. Given the right circumstances, we all have the potential to behave in an unreasonable manner. Most organisations where bullying or harassment occurs have a culture that encourages or fails to stop bad behaviours. Risks such as high levels of stress, poor management styles, or a culture where difference is not accommodated can all contribute to poor behaviours emerging and escalating into bullying or harassment. Focusing only on the perpetrators behaviour, and failing to address the other factors (risk factors) that have contributed to the behaviour is a simplistic and naive way of tackling workplace bullying.

Carlo Caponecchia and Anne Wyatt wrote a very interesting commentary on the problems associated with examining bullying from within this narrow framework, concluding that workplace bullying should be addressed through *'science and risk management rather than alarmist positions of blame and shame '*(p. 406).[17] While all individuals need to be made accountable for their actions, naming and blaming and shaming without identifying and controlling the risk factors that contribute to bad behaviour will do little to prevent the re-emergence of similar problems.

Endnotes

1   Hogh, A., Mikkelsen, E. & Hansen, A.M. (2011). Individual consequences of workplace bullying/mobbing. In S. Einarsen, H. Hoel, D. Zapf, & C. Cooper (Eds.), *Bullying and harassment in the workplace: Developments in theory, research and practice* (2nd ed., pp. 107–122). London, England: CRC Press.

2   Niedl, K. (1996). Mobbing and well-being: Economic and personal development implications. *European Journal of Work and Organizational Behaviour, 5,* 165–184.

3   Traweger, C., Kinzl, J., Traweger-Ravanelli, B., & Fiala, M. (2004). Psychosocial factors in the workplace — Do they affect substance use? Evidence from the Tyrolen workplace study. *Pharmacoepidemiology and Drug Safety, 13,* 399–403.

4   Rayner, C. (1999). From research to implementation: Finding leverage for prevention. *International Journal of Manpower, 20,* 28–38.

5   Vartia, M. (2001). Consequences of workplace bullying with respect to the wellbeing of its targets and the observers of bullying. *Scandinavian Journal of Work Environment and Health, 27,* 63–69.

6   House of representatives Standing Committee on Education and Employment, Workplace Bullying "We Just Want it to Stop", 2012, Canberra.

7   Jenkins, M.F., Winefield, H., & Sarris, A. (2011). Consequences of being accused of workplace bullying: An exploratory study. *International Journal of Workplace Health Management,* 4(1), 33–47; Jenkins, M., Zapf, D., Winefield, H., & Sarris, A. (2011). Bullying allegations from the accused bully's perspective. *British Journal of Management (Online).* doi: 10.1111/j.1467-8551.2011.00778.x

8   Safe Work Australia (2011). Compendium of Workers' Compensation Statistics Australia 2008–2009. Retrieved from http://safeworkaustralia.gov.au

9   Safe Work Australia (2011). Compendium of Workers' Compensation Statistics Australia 2008–2009. Retrieved from http://safeworkaustralia.gov.au

10   *WorkSafe Victoria v Ballarat Radio Pty Ltd* - Ballarat Magistrate's Court (August 2004)

11   *Mckenna v State of Victoria* [1998] VADT 83

12 Café Vamp case. Retrieved from http://www.worksafe.vic.gov.au

13 *Naidu v Group 4 Securitas Pty Ltd & Anor* [2005] NSWSC

14 *Nikolich v Goldman Sachs J B Were Services Pty Ltd* [2006] FCA 784

15 *Goldman Sachs JB Were Services Pty Ltd v Nikolich* [2007]

16 Crawshaw, L. (2010). Coaching abrasive leaders: Using action research to reduce suffering and increase productivity in organisations. *International Journal of Coaching in Organisations, 29* (8), 60-77.

17 Caponecchia, C. & Wyatt, A. (2007). The problem with 'workplace psychopaths'. *Journal of Occupational Health and Safety Australia and New Zealand, 23*(5) 403–405.

PART 2

Assessing the Risks

CHAPTER 4

A Risk Management Approach

Employer Responsibilities

A number of regulatory bodies and OH&S advisory authorities such as Safe Work Australia,[1] WorkSafe Victoria,[2] SafeWork SA,[3] and WorkCover NSW[4] provide recommendations, codes of conduct and guidance on the ways in which employers should manage workplace bullying from within a risk management framework. These recommendations are based on the responsibilities employers have in taking steps to first identify, and then mitigate or manage risks that could contribute to psychological hazards in the workplace, as they would any other OH&S hazard.

As an example of how risk factors can contribute to bullying and harassment at is clearly illustrated by the findings of the enquiry into bullying and harassment within the New South Wales (NSW) Ambulance Service.[5] This enquiry identified a number of cultural and systemic factors that placed employees at risk of bullying. The initial enquiry heard that bullying behaviour was extremely prevalent and little had been done about it. In fact in some parts of the service, bullying was almost viewed as acceptable behaviour by some officers. The bullying had contributed to significant psychological health problems including depression, anxiety and self-harm in a number of personnel. There were a number of submissions from ambulance officers who had contemplated suicide and from families whose members had committed suicide.

The enquiry highlighted the risk factors that had contributed to this culture of workplace bullying. They included:

- A highly dysfunctional environment characterised by low staff morale, high levels of stress and unresolved conflict.
- A nepotistic 'old boys club' that rewarded its own members and penalised those who did not belong.
- Managers who were inept and uncaring and ignored staff problems and policies.
- A culture where management appeared to care more about budgets and performance indicators than employees.
- Poor working conditions and high levels of work stress that were not managed by the organisation.
- An apparent unwillingness or incapacity of managers to deal effectively with staff conflicts, difficult situations or people.
- Victimisation of staff who made complaints through the organisation's grievance processes.
- Significant conflict in some stations between the older staff who were more experienced and the younger staff who had more formal qualifications.
- The 'normalisation' of bullying behaviour by some officers.[6]

These variables all allowed disrespectful behaviours to emerge and escalate into workplace bullying and harassment. An organisation cannot prevent bullying if it fails to identify the presence of these risks, and then allows them to go unchecked. Rather, the OH&S approach to workplace bullying is proactive, and organisations that use this approach have a system in place to assess the presence and degree of risk, and then take steps to control or manage those identified risks, continually monitoring and evaluating the system.

A risk management approach though not traditionally used for sexual harassment and discrimination can also help prevent these behaviours from occurring. Carrying out as many steps as are reasonable in order to prevent bullying and harassment, while not always eliminating all bad behaviours may lessen the impact of the behaviour on a target should bad behaviour occur, because the behaviour is identified and addressed straight away.

> Employers have a legal obligation to do everything reasonably practical to prevent bullying, sexual harassment and discrimination from occurring.

A recent sexual harassment case highlights the importance of organisations implementing a number of strategies to prevent harassment. In the NSW Administrative Decisions Tribunal a male health worker was found guilty of sexually harassing a colleague by giving her a sexually graphic e-mail to read (the e-mail had been sent to another person, but he had obtained a hard copy of it). While the male worker was fined $10,000, the employer escaped liability because the court found that the organisation had taken all the appropriate 'reasonable steps' to prevent the harassment from occurring, and acted swiftly to deal with the incident as soon as it came to their attention. The tribunal found that the steps taken by the employer *'were sufficient, in the sense that al steps that could have been taken were in fact taken'.*[7]

This case can be contrasted with a number of others in this book, in which employers failed to take reasonable steps to prevent the behaviour. It highlights the importance of employers taking as many appropriate and reasonable steps as practical to prevent sexual harassment and workplace bullying.

Hazard — Something that has the potential to harm a person. Hazards at work traditionally were identified as physical things (such as dangerous goods, slippery floors or other 'things'), but psychological threats such as bullying, unacceptable stress and violence are now identified as hazards because of their potential to harm a person.

Risk — The likelihood that a harmful physical or psychological consequence (death, injury or illness) might result when an employee or another person is exposed to a hazard.

Risk management — The processes that are directed at managing adverse effects. In other words, doing something to first remove the risk, and if that is not possible, minimising the risk as much as possible.

Where Do You Start?

The challenge for employers is how to apply the principles of a risk management approach to prevent and address bullying. As traditional risk management systems were designed to identify and eliminate or minimise physical hazards, the concept of psychological hazards can be confusing. In this case, a psychological hazard is a pattern of behaviour or actions that can cause psychological harm or injury to an individual. Risk factors are the workplace characteristics that interact with human activity and have the potential to contribute to psychological hazards such as bullying. Sexual harassment and unlawful discrimination are also potential psychological hazards because both can contribute to psychological injury.

When designing a risk management approach to tackle bullying and harassment, some of the questions that are usually asked are: 'Who should be involved in the design of the system?',

'How do we begin?', 'What do we need to do?'. Unfortunately, it is often the case that organisations only start to develop a proper approach to tackling bullying after the problem has emerged and things have gone badly. However, a risk management approach helps *prevent* the hazard from occurring; it does not wait for bullying to become a problem in the organisation before something is done about it. A risk management approach is proactive.

Management Commitment

The first step is having a strong management commitment to the risk management approach. The organisation's leadership team needs to be motivated to prevent bullying from a systemic and proactive perspective rather than a reactive perspective, or nothing will change. A proper risk management approach to preventing workplace bullying needs to be treated just as seriously by the board of directors, the CEO or executive, as they would treat an approach to managing a physical hazard in the workplace. Employers also need to gain the support of their middle management team and employees, and they need to demonstrate to all of their staff that they are serious about preventing psychological hazards such as bullying and sexual harassment from occurring in their workforce.

Senior management could take the following positive actions to demonstrate their commitment to proper risk management:

Speak to staff about their approach.

- Engage critical stakeholders such as HR Consultants, OH&S representatives, key employees, the organisation's EAP in finding out how the organisation currently manages conflicts, complaints of bullying and sexual harassment.

- Engage the services of an outside consultant such as an organisational psychologist or an organisational conflict management specialist to assist the organisation in carrying out initial climate surveys and workplace risk assessments and in implementing its risk management strategy.

- Attend OH&S meetings and highlight the importance of psychological safety as well as physical safety.

- Involve representatives from the employee trade union, as well as staff union representatives.

- Ensure that there are enough resources (staff and financial resources) to implement a thorough and systemic approach to preventing and addressing workplace bullying and harassment.

- Engage with a university partner to turn the process into 'action research' that can be used as a teaching tool and example of best practice in the future.

A Step-By-Step Process

To make sure that sexual harassment or bullying (the potential hazard) does not occur, an employer needs to do everything that is what the law usually terms 'reasonably practicable' to ensure that the workplace is safe. If a workplace injury occurs as a result of workplace bullying, and the employer is taken to court, they will usually be asked what the organisation has done to *prevent* the behaviour from occurring in the first place. Similarly, if a complaint of sexual harassment or discrimination is lodged with the relevant jurisdiction, and goes to court, the employer will be asked to outline what steps they have taken to *prevent* the behaviour from occurring. The court will want to know that the employer has carried out everything that is reasonably practicable to prevent the bullying or sexual harassment.

SAMPLE SCENARIO

A regulatory authority has taken your organisation to court because an employee has successfully made a claim for a psychological injury caused by workplace bullying and sexual harassment. Your organisation has been accused of failing to protect the worker from workplace bullying and sexual harassment. It is alleged that over a one-year period the worker was bullied, and subjected to inappropriate sexual comments including being sent pornographic pictures. Because of this behaviour, they have suffered a psychological injury. The claimant's psychiatrist has reported that they are suffering from an adjustment disorder, depression and anxiety because of workplace bullying and sexual harassment. They have been off work now for 9 months, and argue that the workplace is not safe for them to return.

You have been summoned to appear, and the prosecutor asks you: 'Prior to the complaint, what steps had your organisation put in place to assess the risks of bullying?'. She goes onto ask: 'What steps have you carried out to prevent workplace bullying and sexual harassment from occurring?'.

How would you answer?

There are four steps that employers need to carry out to comply with a risk management approach to preventing and managing bullying as a hazard:

1. **Identify the hazard**. What are we dealing with? Employers need to have a good understanding about what *is* bullying and what *is not* bullying. How bullying, sexual harassment and discrimination link.

2. **Assess the risks.** Employers need to have a good understanding of the risks factors that may be present in their organisation, or discrete pockets of their organisation, and the degree of risk posed by each of the factors identified.
3. **Implement control measures.** Employers need to know what strategies they need to implement in order to minimise and control the risks that they have identified.
4. **Evaluate and review control measures.** Employers need to know how to evaluate the strategies they have put in place, so that they can tell if these control measures have been effective.

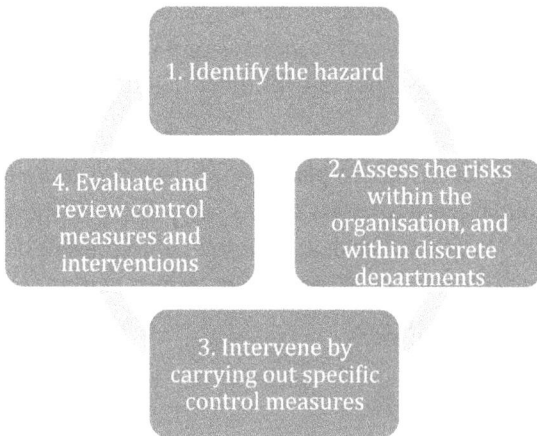

Figure 4.1
A risk management approach to preventing and managing bullying and harassment.[9]

Endnotes

1   Safe Work Australia. (2011). *Preventing and responding to workplace bullying draft code of practice, 2011.* Sydney, Australia: Author.

2   WorkSafe Victoria (2003), *Guidance note on the prevention of bullying and violence at work.* Melbourne, Australia: Author.

3   *Preventing workplace bullying. A practical guide for employers and employees.* Interagency Roundtable on Workplace Bullying, 2005, Adelaide, South Australia.

4   WorkCover NSW. (2008). Preventing and dealing with workplace bullying: A guide for employers and employees. Sydney, Australia: Author.

5   New South Wales Parliament Legislative Council. General Purpose Standing Committee No.2. *The management and operations of the NSW Ambulance Service* [Report]. Retrieved from http://www.parliament.nsw.gov.au/Prod/parlment/committee.nsf/0/b719a16df5b974ebc a2574e7007f68d4/$FILE/FINAL%20REPORT.pdf/

6   New South Wales Parliament Legislative Council. General Purpose Standing Committee No.2. *The management and operations of the NSW Ambulance Service* [Report]. Retrieved from http://www.parliament.nsw.gov.au/Prod/parlment/committee.nsf/0/b719a16df5b974ebc a2574e7007f68d4/$FILE/FINAL%20REPORT.pdf/

7   *Cooper v Western Area local Health Network* [2012] NSWADT 39

8   Adapted from the terms used in: Standards Australia. HB 205-2004, *OHS Risk Management Handbook, Standards Australia,* Sydney, NSW, Australia. (2004)

9   Adapted from 'The four step process'. In *Preventing workplace bullying: A practical guide for employers* (p. 5). Interagency Round Table on Workplace Bullying, Adelaide, South Australia.

CHAPTER 5

Identifying Your Risks

Bullying is symptomatic of broader problems in the work environment and happens within a specific context when individuals feel they need to exert their control, and do so (either intentionally or unintentionally) in an unreasonable manner. Studies have identified several risk factors that can contribute to bullying. A risk management approach involves identifying the presence of these risks, evaluating the impact of the risks on the organisation and either eliminating or controlling them. Organisations that focus only on the relationship between the target and perpetrator fail to recognise that the poor behaviours exhibited by the perpetrator (and sometimes both parties) could not have occurred if the environment or culture had not been permissive of the behaviours. When taking a risk management approach, it is recommended that an organisation assess each department individually to determine the risk of poor behaviours occurring in isolated parts of the organisation.

The research has identified six main classes of risk for bullying.

• Industrial climate and work organisation
• Significant changes within the organisation
• The social environment
• Leadership styles
• Characteristics of targets and perpetrators
• Lack of systems and policies

In this chapter, these classes of risks are discussed, with examples from case studies to illustrate how they may have contributed to the bullying or harassment. Workplace bullying, and harassment usually occur because of an interaction between some of these risk factors, and is less likely to occur if these factors are identified in the organisation as potential risks and are controlled or managed effectively. For example, employees are less likely to bully or sexually harass other employees if the organisation has policies in relation to respectful workplace behaviour, all employees have had training on their rights and responsibilities and workgroup managers are proactive in early intervention and addressing inappropriate behaviour that they witness or hear about. Managers are less likely to bully employees if they are aware that their own poor behaviour will not be tolerated, and if they have had training on how to manage employee performance according to the reasonable standards and frameworks set down by the organisation. On the other hand bullying is more likely to occur in organisations that have issues such as understaffing, employees with ambiguous roles and reporting structures, departments where significant changes are causing high levels of stress and where marginalised workers feel isolated and are not allowed to fit in.

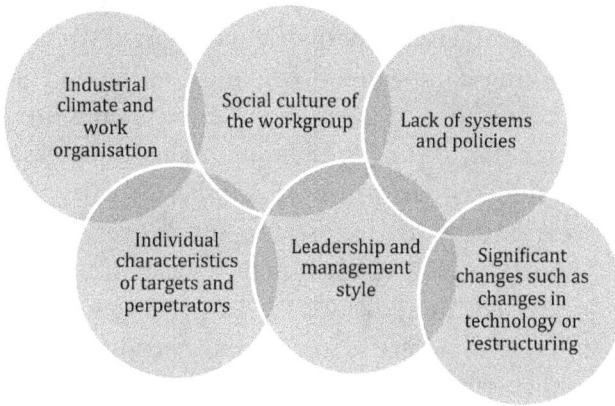

Figure 5.1
Risk factors for workplace bullying.

Industrial Climate and Work Organisation

Studies have shown that both targets and observers of bullying are likely to report high levels of confusion about their roles and their jobs, as well as perceptions of contradictory expectations, demands and goals. In examining more than a decade of bullying research, one study found that bullying tended to occur in work environments where stressors such as competing job demands, expectations from others, role ambiguity (not being sure about what jobs you are required to carry out), role overload (too many tasks and not enough time to carry them all out) and lack of autonomy (being dependent on others in order to carry out your own job) were present. Role conflict and ambiguity were found to be the strongest predictors of workplace bullying in this study, as well as lack of control over work environment.[1]

The interviews that I conducted as part of my doctoral research confirmed many of these findings. My interviews with targets of bullying, and alleged perpetrators, illustrated that bullying often occurred in negative and stressful working environments. Both targets and perpetrators reported stressful and negative working conditions, with role conflict and uncertainty also contributing to the bullying. For example, one team leader reported that at the time a bullying allegation was made against her, she was performing a number of roles that she believed were outside her job description because of significant staff shortages and changes taking place in the hospital where she worked. In addition, she was trying to manage a team of nurses who were also stressed and displaying bad behaviours themselves. She described herself as being anxious and stressed and said that staff had told her that she was becoming aggressive. She said:

> What happened in the beginning was that we were having a lot of trouble with our workplace ... The staff weren't happy with the lack of staffing and resources that we had. There were no doctors to support them. I was also finding it a very stressful time myself because the workload was huge. My job really should have been done by two people ... I started having to cover for doctors as well, so I didn't have doctors in the emergency department, I didn't have doctors seeing mental health patients on the wards and I had to do both in each area. The nursing staff said that wasn't appropriate that I do that, and I said, 'well I know it's not, but it's all we have'. I also had the management aspect of my job, and so I was working long hours ...

> People started to comment that I was getting aggressive, and I said, 'Well, what do you mean by that?' They are saying, 'Oh, you are just very short with us all the time', and I'm saying, 'Well, I don't mean to be; I don't notice that I am', and I would say to them that I am getting tired ... There was a particular day where this nurse told me that they didn't support me anymore ... That was quite devastating because I thought that I was a good boss. They had more than any other team had in terms of education. I was always looking for them and

sending them off to do some courses and things like that. I was always acknowledging that it was difficult for them. I would go over and I would help them out, so I felt that I was doing all I could. However, he made it very clear that that's not how they felt, and so I was in tears after that. I got up, and I left, and I said, 'Right, well, I'm leaving now. I'm not going to continue with this conversation', and I left, and I went back to my office, and I was quite upset.

Significant Changes

As well as staffing problems and role ambiguity, other organisational stressors that can contribute to bullying emerging in an organisation include significant changes in the workplace such as downsizing, restructuring and the introduction of new systems, procedures or technology. Many of these risk factors are unavoidable, but if managed correctly their impact on staff minimised. Large changes can affect individuals and contribute to increased levels of stress, conflict and defensive behaviours among staff. If they are not managed properly, these poor behaviours can escalate into bullying.

During times there may be greater job insecurity, uncertainty and lack of autonomy as changes are implemented. Workers may be less likely to complain about inappropriate behaviours for fear of losing their jobs. When managers are anxious, their conflict style also tends to become reactive and autocratic rather than explanatory or negotiating. Anxious people often interpret neutral events in the environment (such as a failure to say hello) as threatening. This can contribute to heightened conflict and the emergence of reactive negative behaviours. Workers need significant support and clear communication from management with consistent messages to support them during stressful transitions.

Social Environment

Organisational social environments are the expectations, beliefs and standards that group members come to share and take for granted. A workgroup environment can differentiate itself from the wider organisational environment when attitudes and behaviours that may not be acceptable in the wider organisation may be established in isolated pockets of the organisation. The difficulty that group members have in complaining about inappropriate behaviours illustrates the potential strength of social processes that occur within discrete workgroups. The way that targets react to the group behaviour can further isolate them from the work group where the inappropriate behaviours are considered the norm. Conflict with group norms has been found to be a significant cause of workplace bullying, and predatory bullying can occur in situations where a social group or a member of a dominant group targets a new group member because they do not fit in. Targets complaining about or challenging inappropriate group norms may be stigmatised and find it more difficult to become part of the group, exacerbating their isolation and victimisation. This type of predatory bullying towards individuals who challenge established social norms has led to a number of court cases in Australia; for example, where women were bullied or sexually harassed when they did not fit into the norms of male-dominated industries such as mining.[2] In a similar manner, there have been sexual harassment complaints by women targeted by a group that has 'normalised' a sexualised workplace culture within an organisation. Many perpetrators will only bully or harass others in a workgroup if the social environment of the group allows or encourages such behaviour. Managers have a responsibility to prevent the development of an inappropriate culture within their teams, and stopping inappropriate behaviours that they become aware of. Organisational cultures where 'initiation' practices for new workers or apprentices occur, not only present a physical OH&S risk in themselves but can also lead to bullying when those workers who do not want to be subjected to such practices are punished through exclusion and bullying.

Frank's story: An example of a sexualised social environment

(Note the overlap between bullying and sexual harassment and the use of technology to promote the sexualised work environment.)

> One of them would get some disgusting pornographic short videos and show them on their phones. Then they would show each other and then transfer it to each other's phones via Bluetooth and the videos — a couple of them that I did see, that I was shown — they were absolutely disgusting. They were just nothing short of this violent erotica. They were just absolutely degrading to women, absolutely appalling that anyone would get any gratification out of watching that sort of thing, and I would just tell them all the time that they had a real problem, and how anyone gets any satisfaction or gratification at all seeing that sort of thing. They said that I must have been a poof because I found it disgusting. They said that I must be homosexual if I didn't find it really good and look at all of these things. I would complain to the boss about this and he said, 'Oh yes, they do it all the time …'

In this example, Frank was describing a sexualised social environment where pornography was the norm and most of the male employees distributed and read pornography. However, when Frank complained about it, his boss normalised the behaviour as something they do all the time, and the employees singled Frank out because he did not participate in the behaviours, calling him a 'homosexual' because he did not want to participate in the behaviour.

In the case *Horman v Distribution Group*[3], Ms Horman complained of inappropriate comments and behaviours such as writing on her body with a felt-tip pen, pulling her bra straps and touching her buttocks She only complained about the behaviour after she was made redundant and left the workplace. During the court case, the organisation argued that she was a willing participant in this behaviour and actually instigated some of it herself. The organisation told the court that they had an equal opportunity policy and complaints procedure, but Ms Horman had not followed them or made any complaint during her employment. While they agreed that there was some 'horse-play' in the workplace, they said that Ms Horman was a willing participant in these activities and that she also used crude language and engaged in similar behaviour to the others in the workgroup. However, the magistrate found that a reasonable person in Ms Horman's position would have been offended, humiliated or intimidated by the behaviours and remarks in the workplace, despite the fact that she had participated in some of them. He found that management had allowed the behaviour to go on and actually participated in it themselves. The magistrate said that:

> I am not sure that a reasonable person would not anticipate that the applicant would be offended, humiliated or intimi-dated by bad language solely because the applicant herself also used it from time to time. 'Giving as good as you get' is often the only way in which a person feels he or she can resist unpleasant language and would not to my mind indicate to a reasonable person the type of acceptance of the language which would relieve a respondent of liability.

This case illustrates how an inappropriate workplace culture or social environment can lead to complaints of bullying, sexual harassment or discrimination. It also illustrates how some targets of bullying or sexual harassment might also act badly themselves, 'giving as good as they get', in order to survive an inappropriate culture. Because management participated in the behaviour described by Ms Horman and condoned it, she was not able to complain and may have participated in order to 'fit in' with the group. The magistrate made the point that even though she had participated in the sexualised behaviours, it did not mean she would not be offended, humiliated or intimidated by some of the actions and remarks that were made. The magistrate said, 'I found that everyone was entitled to draw the line somewhere, and those activities crossed the line'.

A workforce that contains vulnerable workers who are different from the wider workforce may be particularly at risk. Vulnerable workers have attributes or characteristics that place them in a minority, such as women working in a male-dominated workforce, younger workers or apprentices, workers from overseas who are not used to working in a western culture and workers with a mental illness or a disability. Workers in remote or isolated geographical areas may also be at greater risk because of their isolation. All of these factors can contribute to inappropriate behaviours going undetected and are significant risk factors for workplace bullying.

The case of *Lee v Smith and Others*[4] highlights the serious consequences of organisations not taking measures to ensure that the workplace is safe from potential hazards such as sexual harassment and workplace bullying. A culture in which sexual harassment and workplace bullying occur unchecked can lead to significant injury for targets.

The complainant claimed that she was sexually harassed and bullied, and that the inappropriate behaviours were not addressed when she complained. She alleged that the failure of her employer to stop the sexual harassment, contributed to her being raped by a colleague one night after a dinner party. However, when she complained about this at work, she alleged that she was bullied and further victimised by the organisation, which minimised her concerns as 'personal problems', and failed to adequately address the behaviours of the perpetrator.' As you read the following information, think about the risk factors that were present in the organisation that contributed to the behaviours that the target was subjected to.

Lee v Smith and Others

Cassandra was employed in an administrative position. In her complaint, she alleged that there were calendars of topless women and computer images containing pornography readily visible as she moved about the workplace. She also alleged that one of her colleagues sexually harassed her during a computer course that they attended. She told the court that after the course, when they were waiting to go back to their workplace he said to her that he would like to have sex with her. She said that when she rejected his advances, he said, 'you will be sorry', in a threatening tone. She described a workplace culture where sexual innuendos and comments appeared to be the norm. The inappropriate, sexually harassing behaviours became common in the workplace and worsened over time.

Cassandra told the court that she went to the home of some fellow employees for dinner, where she became intoxicated and fell asleep on the couch. She alleged that when she awoke the following morning around daybreak, she was naked from the waist down and a colleague was having sex with her. She said that he later made a number of threats to her if she revealed what had occurred, including using his influence at work to drive her from the workplace. She alleged that after she had reported the rape and sexual harassment, the employer was not at all supportive. She said that rather than addressing the allegations, she was counselled about her poor performance and criticised for bringing her personal problems to work. She gave an example of being publicly humiliated in the workplace each day by a list of tasks given to her and placed on her desk in a very prominent position where other staff could see. She also had work go missing and was counselled about her poor performance without good reason.

In this case, the court found that:

- The rape was the culmination of the earlier incidents of sexual harassment directly in the workplace. Consequently, the respondent's conduct was an extension or continuation of his pattern of behaviour that had started and continued to develop in the workplace. The relationship between the rape at a colleague's house, and the workplace was not broken.

- The employer was under an obligation to take all reasonable steps to prevent the rape but failed in this obligation by not implementing correct policies. While the employer had detailed, comprehensive and appropriate equity and diversity policies, they were not followed.

- Cassandra had not received any training in how to address sexual harassment. This was found to be a failure of the employer to take all reasonable steps to prevent the sexual harassment and rape, so the employer was held to be vicariously liable.

The magistrate also accepted that Cassandra's line managers had victimised and bullied her following the sexual harassment and rape allegations. This included yelling at her, setting tasks that were too difficult to achieve and recommending and completing performance counselling when it was not warranted.

This case highlights that managers and organisations can be found liable for the behaviour of individuals within the organisation, even if that behaviour occurs outside the workplace. The findings of this case were appealed by the organisation but were upheld. In the judgement handed following the appeal, the court increased the payment to Cassandra Lee from $100,000 to $400,000, with the cost to be paid equally by all respondents. The breakdown of payments was:

- Compensation $100,000
- Special Damages $232,163
- Medical costs $25,259
- Lost Wages $30,000.

If the organisation had addressed the risks that were present in the environment prior to the hazardous behaviours occurring, implemented its relevant policies and provided staff training, the situation that Cassandra found herself in may have been prevented.

The strong messages from this case are, firstly, that managers cannot be indifferent to inappropriate workplace cultures, and other risks present in the environment that might contribute to bullying or harassment. Inappropriate behaviours can have a significant negative impact on individuals both at work, and outside the workplace. Secondly, it is important for organisations to focus on addressing the complaint, rather than victimising the person who is complaining. Finally, a person who has a psychological injury because of workplace bullying, sexual harassment or victimisation may be behaving erratically (due to their injury), but they require support and care. The potential risk of inappropriate workplace cultures reinforces the need for all managers to address unacceptable behaviour before that behaviour contributes to an employee being injured.

Leadership Styles

An autocratic manager, who exerts their authority inappropriately, may be bullying their staff even if this is not intentional. There are times when is perfectly reasonable for a manager to be direct; however, managers who as the norm, exclude workers in the decision-making process, use punishment as a form of management and rule through intimidation can be bullying staff through their autocratic management style. Often the controlling manager does not realise that some their behaviours may be bullying, and will justify them as 'reasonable management practice', and their staff as too sensitive. However, this style of management can be bullying, as illustrated in Suzette's story.

Suzette's story: The authoritarian manager

... then she came in and virtually stripped our office of everything without asking. All our notes came off the wall. She just did it, cleaned the office up when we weren't there. All of our postcards from our holidays off the wall. She wasn't interested in your opinion ... Then she decided that she would do staff evaluation interviews after being there two weeks, which I thought was surprising. She gave us all a form to fill in about ourselves. Quite personal information about our home life, which I thought was inappropriate ... By this stage, people were getting a bit 'pissed off' with her and her attitude ... every girl that came out of her interview came out sobbing, and they would run off into the toilet ... She had called another couple of girls in and torn strips off them like they were schoolgirls ... she said, 'Well, I am the practice manager here and everyone will just do as I say'. She said, 'Sit down'. I said, 'No, I don't want to sit down'. She said, 'When I tell you to sit down, you sit down. I am your boss ...'

Suzette's story describes a manager with an authoritarian style, who managed through fear and intimidation. According to Suzette, the practice manager viewed herself as 'the boss' and did not to want to enter into discussions with staff or take into account how her own behaviour affected them. It appears that much of the bullying occurred behind closed doors, where the girls 'came out sobbing'. The manager would also carry out unreasonable behaviours when other staff members and witnesses were not present. Despite Suzette complaining to the director of the medical practice, the new manager's actions were supported because the directors felt that the nurses and reception staff needed a manager as the practice was growing. The 'bully' managed to convince the directors that the staff were rebelling against reasonable management practices, and that a tough management approach was needed because they had been without management direction previously. When I talked to Suzette, she said that the surgery did not have a bullying policy, and she did not think that the directors knew what bullying was or what their responsibilities were in relation to psychological safety at work. Suzette said nobody had received any training in regard to their rights or responsibilities in this area. The management style of the bully was normalised as 'tough management'. Unfortunately, the tactics used by the new manager resulted in high levels of staff sick leave, and three staff members resigning (including Suzette).

Despite the scarcity of research into bullies, managers are reported to be the most frequent bully perpetrators, and it has been recognised that bullying behaviours can be a deliberate means by some managers to influence others to achieve personal and organisational goals. In these workplaces, the focus is on the financial bottom line, and the human side of management is given a lesser priority. Bullying in this light is seen as a legitimate managerial prerogative. Some managers may unintentionally bully in this way, failing to understand the target's perspective instead focusing on justifying their own behaviour. However, lack of intention by the perpetrator does not mean that their repeated unreasonable behaviours are not bullying.

On the other hand, laissez faire management style has been referred to as nonmanagement. Laissez faire managers fail to address problems in their team and leave problems for their workers to resolve. They want to be liked by their team, and want to be part of the team rather than a leader. Some laissez faire managers are intimidated by members of their team and so do not get involved when there is conflict or inappropriate behaviours. They often delegate all of their managerial responsibilities to others and do not get involved. Managers who are very slack or have a laissez faire attitude can also contribute to workplace bullying because they fail to properly supervise or guide workers, provide adequate feedback, or address poor performance or behaviour problems. Some manager actually encourage inappropriate behaviours through their own actions.

If a manager is trying to be 'mates' with the workers who are behaving badly, it is almost impossible for a target to make a complaint and have it addressed seriously. One manager who I interviewed as part of my doctoral research (who had been found guilty of bullying and sexual harassment) made the following comment to me:

> I am very professional when need be, but when there is no one in the office I kind of make it a very casual environment, which is kind of how we achieve our best work ... Sometimes I can call it kind of like a pub environment for want of a better word because it is very laid back and casual'. (Middle Manager, private industry)

His comments suggest that he supported and promoted a workplace environment that permitted inappropriate behaviours. He appeared to have little insight into how inappropriate his own behaviour was and defended it by saying that he was professional when he needed to be, but when no clients were present, he promoted a 'pub environment'. He was dismissed from his job after he sent around photos in which he had Photoshopped penises and vomit on the images of various staff members. He had also sent around homophobic jokes to various staff members. He could not understand why his employment had been terminated, and told me that he did not mean to harm anyone, and the images he distributed were jokes. He took his employer to court for unfair dismissal but lost the case.

Characteristics of Targets and Perpetrators

When discussing target's characteristics as contributing to bullying, it is important not to blame them, but to draw attention to the reason that they may be bullied. The bullying literature has quashed the legitimacy of a typical 'victim personality'. However, the literature does point out that sometimes the behaviours or the characteristics of the target have placed them at risk of workplace bullying[5].

Some targets may be at greater risk because they are different from the typical employees in the group. For example, their personality, interests, sexuality, race, religious beliefs or work ethic could place them at a higher risk of being treated unreasonably because they do not fit in to the group, making them 'one of them', not 'one of us'. These targets often do nothing to provoke the behaviour to which they are exposed. Sometimes target characteristics are covered by equal opportunity and anti-discrimination laws. Sometimes they are not. However, irrespective of whether target characteristics fall under anti-discrimination legislation, if unreasonable and threatening behaviour is repeated and has the potential to cause harm, it can be classified as workplace bullying.

Targets do not very often acknowledge that their own behaviour might have triggered the bullying. However, some targets might invite bullying behaviour by provoking anger or retaliatory behaviours in others. This group of targets might behave in a way that makes them vulnerable to retaliation or victimisation. This group includes the whistleblowers, employees whose personality makes them want to dominate or employees whose actions challenge others in authority or power. Employees who work harder and are more diligent (and are therefore a threat to others) or who have poor conflict management skills might also provoke retaliation from others. People who become defensive in the face of perceived threat, or those who find it difficult to manage their own emotions in a constructive way may be more likely to be both targets of bullying and perpetrators. All of these employee characteristics need to be managed in a fair and transparent manner. Retaliation is not a justification for bullying. Bad behaviour managed by even worse behaviour is a recipe for workplace bullying.

Some bullying is the result of conflict escalation and emerges from unresolved workplace conflicts or high levels of constant pressure where one or both parties are not coping.

Bullying is a method used by some individuals to gain control of their environment, and all humans have the capacity to behave badly when they are stressed or confronted by intense pressure, or when their mental and physical resources are stretched to the limit. Some bullies might vent their frustrations or anger at vulnerable individuals because of their own lack of emotional regulation and stress management skills. Many bullies are poor self-reflectors and may not be fully aware of how their behaviour is affecting others. However, as discussed earlier, intentionality is not part of bullying or sexual harassment definitions. A perpetrator may not intend to bully or harass someone, but if their behaviour meets the definition, and it is reasonable under the circumstances that the target felt threatened, then it may be bullying. In a study I carried out as part of my doctorial research,[6] most bullies had very little insight into the effects of their behaviour on others around them. All the accused bullies reported that they did not intend to hurt anyone. Some justified their behaviour as 'jokes' or 'sense of humour' claiming that the complainants misinterpreted their actions. Others reported that their behaviour as justifiable and reasonable management actions. While 90% of research participants reported that they had *never* bullied anyone, and 10% reported that they had bullied someone on a *rare occasion*, 26% had bullying allegations against them substantiated. These results suggest that sometimes managers may not realise that the way they do things is unreasonable and perceived as threatening by the recipient.

Some studies also suggest that displaced aggression can also contribute to bullying.[7] Displaced aggression refers to a tendency for employees to act out against a junior person in authority (i.e., their team leader or junior manager) because it is unsafe to retaliate against a senior authority figure (e.g., the CEO or owner of the business). This displaced aggression may be responsible for what we know as 'upwards bullying'; that is, middle managers or managers bullied by their subordinates. It may be safer for a worker to bully his or her own manger, than retaliate against the CEO or a more senior manager.

Lack of Systems and Policies

A lack of systems and policies or the failure to implement established systems or policies supports an environment for an ongoing culture of inherent bad behaviours, and also leaves the organisation open to legal proceedings under relevant state or federal legislation. A policy aimed at preventing bullying, sexual harassment and discrimination provides employees, including managers, with rules and guidelines to ensure that work employees act in a manner that meets the organisation's standards of behaviour and is consistent with legal standards of conduct. A policy is an organisation's position or stance on a particular issue. A policy is enforceable, which means that breaches of the policy may incur disciplinary action.

Respectful behaviour policies that link to an organisation's code of conduct, performance management policies, return-to-work policies, sick leave policies, OH&S policies and a number of other organisational directives, are very important for the ongoing 'health' of the organisation. There should be a system in place in which all employees are made aware of their obligations and their rights. An organisation that does not have a policy that provides clear direction to employees on how to behave or what to do in a variety of situations potentially has a number of problems. The first is that employees are able to say that they do not know what their rights or obligations are in relation to standards of behaviour within the organisation. No standard has been set. The worst-case scenario is that the employer is left open to legal action if an employee is injured at work and there is no policy directing staff not to behave in an a way that contributed to the injury.

Employees and managers need consistent feedback addressing both their strengths as well as the areas of performance that are challenging. Part of employee or manager performance includes their communication style, ability to work within a team and their leadership/management style. Often these aspects of performance management are overlooked in favour of the more technical aspects of the positions. Performance management systems that link in with other policies allow behaviours to be monitored and addressed if needed. Performance management policies need to link with the organisation's training and development policies so that employees and managers are able to obtain coaching, training and mentoring in the areas identified as challenging or needing improvement.

Many organisations have policies that are not accessible, used or adhered to. They sit on a shelf gathering dust, or lie buried in the organisation's intranet. Policies need to part of an organisation's system of communication to their employees. Policies need to be easily accessible and understood by all staff. Managers need to know what their obligations are in preventing complaints of workplace bullying and harassment, and how to address verbal and written allegations. Employees need to know where they can go, and what their options are if things go wrong. Policies are living and evolving documents that need to be kept up to date in order to keep pace with the changes in information technology, industrial legislation, anti-discrimination and OH&S laws.

The risk factors described in this chapter often do not produce bullying on their own but interact with each other to contribute to the development and escalation of poor behaviours. If not identified and addressed early, these behaviours escalate into bullying and other types hazardous workplace activities. Therefore, HR practitioners, managers and organisation development specialists need identify risks in the environment that may contribute to the emergence of bullying behaviour, and take steps to control or minimise those risks. If an organisation fails to address bullying from within this systemic approach, it is difficult to prevent bad behaviour from developing and escalating.

Endnotes

1 Bowling, N.A., & Beehr, T.A. (2006). Workplace harassment from the victim's perspective: A theoretical model and meta-analysis. *Journal of Applied Psychology, 91*(5), 998–1012.

2 *Hopper v Mount Isa Mines Ltd*, Queensland Anti-Discrimination Tribunal (1997).

3 *Horman v Distribution Group Ltd*, FMCA 52 (2001).

4 *Lee v Smith & Ors*, FMCA 59 (23 March 2007).

5 Zapf, D. & Einarsen, S. (2011). Individual antecedents of bullying: Victims and perpetrators. In *Bullying and harassment in the workplace: Developments in theory, research and practice* (2nd ed., pp. 177–201). London, England: CRC Press.

6 Jenkins, M., Zapf, D., Winefield, H., & Sarris, A. (2011). Bullying allegations from the accused bully's perspective. *British Journal of Management (Online).* doi: 10.1111/j.1467-8551.2011.00778.x

7 Marcus-Newhall, A., Pedersen, W.C., & Miller, N. (2000). Displaced aggression is live and well: A meta-analytic review. *Journal of Personality and Social Psychology, 78,* 670–689.

CHAPTER 6

Workplace Risk Assessment

Determining Specific Risk

The first part of preventing workplace bullying from an OH&S perspective is to assess the prevalence of risks that might be present in the organisation or specific department. Risk assessments need to be connected to the specific risks that have been identified as contributing to workplace bullying. The assessment findings then lead into specific control measures, or ways of managing the identified risks.

The first part of identifying risks within the organisation is communication with all stakeholders. Stakeholders include unions, OH&S representatives and specialists, employees and any other party that will encourage workers to understand the organisations efforts to improve performance in the area. Consultation and collaboration between stakeholders will assist in developing a climate of ownership within the organisation and will illustrate that management and executive are commit-

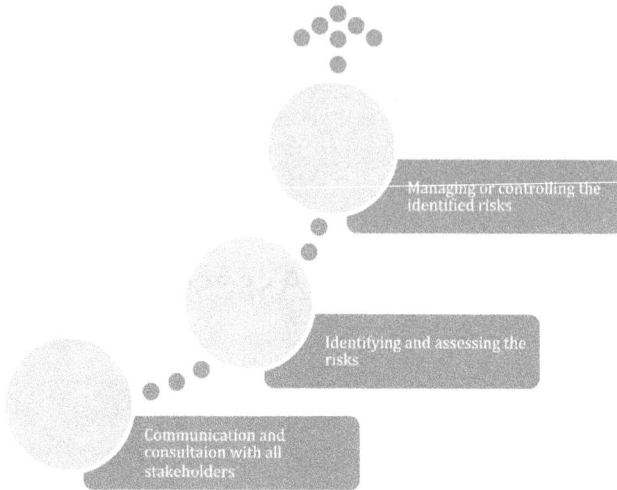

Figure 6.1
The risk assessment process.

ted to this process of improving psychological safety. In order to ensure an effective consultation process an organisation should:

- develop procedures that enable stakeholders to share relevant information, communicate effectively and have genuine input into the process

- ensure information from stakeholders is fed back to employees throughout the consultation process

- develop a process that provides employees and other stakeholders the ability to express their views and contribute to improving psychological safety.

By working through a risk assessment tool like the one outlined in this chapter, an organisation can identify areas within the workplace that might create a risk to health and safety through bullying and other inappropriate conduct. The tool may help to identify particular departments that are at greater risk, and specific gaps in training, policy or job design. It important to note however, that a specific risk management tool is not a stand-alone method of risk assessment. A risk assessment tool is insufficient in itself to conduct a full assessment of the risks present in an organisation. Stand-alone checklists can be problematic and provide a false sense of security when used as the only tool for identifying risks. A risk assessment framework is dynamic and involves a continuous process. A review of the risks needs to be systematic and involve consultation with managers and employees at all levels of the organisation.

Standards Australia[i] highlight the importance of risk management activities being applied at all levels of the organisation. This means that risk management in relation psychological injury needs to start at a strategic level where the organisation addresses how psychological hazards (as well as physical hazards) might affect the overall objectives of the organisation. Part of this strategic approach examines how the management of psychological hazards fits into the current OH&S strategy of the organisation. Establishing and monitoring resources (both financial and personnel) needed to implement a psychological safety management system, and incorporating a risk management approach to identifying and preventing psychological hazards is also an important component of corporate governance.

On an operational level risk management is linked to the day-to-day activities of the organisation. Whoever is in charge of the risk management process must:

- Conduct exit interviews with all staff to ascertain why they are leaving.

- Examine sick leave, staff turnover, and workers compensation claim statistics to identify areas that may be experiencing high levels of stress, or high rates of injury.

- Review bullying and harassment 'Contact Officer' statistics, and learning from incidents.

- Manage specific risks in a certain area where risks have been identified.

- Follow up feedback from 'workplace bullying and harassment awareness' training sessions.
- Regularly carry out tailored climate surveys throughout your organisation to identify any concerns staff have about behaviours in their department.

A risk management process is a practice of continual improvement, and is repeated over and over again, modified as needed following input and evaluation.

Policies, Procedures and Culture
Risks in relation to organisational policies, procedures and culture

Does your organisation have an up-to-date policy that sets out standards of acceptable behaviour and defines bullying, sexual harassment and unlawful discrimination as potential workplace hazards?

(Yes/No/Not Sure)

Does your organisation have a documented procedure for addressing complaints of workplace bullying, sexual harassment and discrimination?

(Yes/No/Not Sure)

Has your organisation appointed and trained contact persons to whom aggrieved employees can go and talk about their concerns?

(Yes/No/Not Sure)

Do these contact persons understand their role and how to properly deal with an aggrieved employee?

(Yes/No/Not Sure)

Do your current policies reflect the current OH&S legislation and anti-discrimination laws?

(Yes/No/Not Sure)

Do your policies provide for conflicts that do not reach the threshold of workplace bullying?

(Yes/No/Not Sure)

Have all managers received training on their responsibilities to prevent and manage complaints of bullying, sexual harassment and discrimination? Has the organisation kept records of this training?

(Yes/No/Not Sure)

Have all managers received training on merit based promotion and recruitment processes? Has the organisation kept records of this training?

(Yes/No/Not Sure)

Have all employees received training on their rights and responsibilities in relation to bullying, sexual harassment and discrimination? Has the organisation kept records of this training?

(Yes/No/Not Sure)

Does your organisation have a performance management policy and system of addressing poor performance? Have all managers and supervisors with line management responsibility received training in how to manage employee performance?

(Yes/No/Not Sure)

If you answered NO or Not Sure to any of the above questions, you may need to do one or more of the following in order to control this risk:

- In consultation with staff and OH&S representatives, develop a respectful behaviour policy (incorporating directives on equal opportunity, sexual harassment and workplace bullying).

- Provide mandatory training for all staff and managers that is specifically aimed at their rights and responsibilities in relation to your respectful behaviour policy.

- Provide all new employees with a copy of the policy and information about their rights and responsibilities.

- Ensure contact persons are appointed and trained to carry out their role.

- Have a complaint process that includes early no-blame resolution processes as well as formal processes, so employees can have grievances addressed fairly and quickly.

- Develop a performance management policy and provide training for all managers on how to manage employee performance.
- Provide training for all managers on merit based recruitment and promotion.

Change Management Processes and Work Systems
Risks in relation to organisational changes and work systems

Has there been any or are you expecting any changes in the way work is carried out (such as new technology, new processes or new equipment)?

(Yes/No/Not Sure)

Has there been any significant restructuring in your organisation?

(Yes/No/Not Sure)

Are there staff shortages or departments where workload may be contributing to high levels of stress?

(Yes/No/Not Sure)

Does every employee have an up-to-date and current job description that reflects their current job?

(Yes/No/Not Sure)

Are the job requirements of employees able to accommodate their needs in relation to diversity in the workforce?

(Yes/No/Not Sure)

Are there any foreseeable changes that might affect job security or stability, or create uncertainty among employees?

(Yes/No/Not Sure)

Are all employees confident about their job tenure and security?
(Yes/No/Not Sure)

If you answered YES or NOT SURE to any of these questions, you may need to do one or more of the following in order to control this risk:

- Communicate on a regular basis with all employees about proposed changes and let them have an input as to how these changes are implemented.
- Seek and act on employee feedback regarding any changes.
- Provide any extra training or support needed for workers to adapt to any proposed changes.
- Ensure that you have adequate staff to cover each shift and that staff are in control of their workload with adequate breaks.
- Implement flexible working arrangements, if reasonable, to accommodate the needs of employees.
- Ensure all workers and managers have an up-to-date job description that clearly outlines roles and responsibilities.

Management Styles
Risks in relation to management styles

Have you carried out a culture survey to assess how employees feel about the management culture of your organisation?

(Yes/No/Not Sure)

Do your employees report that any managers or supervisors in their departments have an authoritarian or overbearing leadership style?

(Yes/No/Not Sure)

Do your employees report that any managers or supervisors in their departments have a slack or 'hands-off' approach?

(Yes/No/Not Sure)

Do any employees criticise their manager's interpersonal skills?
(Yes/No/Not Sure)

(Yes/No/Not Sure)

Do you consider your managers have adequate leadership training?

(Yes/No/Not Sure)

Do your managers consider they have had sufficient training in performance management?

(Yes/No/Not Sure)

Do your managers think that they receive adequate supervision and support themselves?

(Yes/No/Not Sure)

Do you think all of your managers would know what to do if an employee complained of conduct that could be potentially harmful, such as bullying, discrimination or sexual harassment?

(Yes/No/Not Sure)

Have all your managers had conflict resolution training? Do they need up-to-date training?

(Yes/No/Not Sure)

Do your managers know what their legal obligations are in relation to preventing and managing workplace bullying?

(Yes/No/Not Sure)

If you could not confidently answer the questions in this section, it might be necessary to conduct a formal survey on management culture in your organisation. You also may need to do one or more of the following in order to control risk arising from poor management styles:

- Provide all managers and leaders with adequate training in communication, leadership and performance management.
- Use coaching and mentoring to improve their management capabilities.
- Provide opportunities for 360-degree feedback for managers from their staff.
- Provide regular training (at least once a year) to ensure that all managers are aware of their responsibilities in terms of preventing and managing workplace bullying, discrimination and harassment.

- Implement performance reviews and regular supervision for managers that include positive behavioural indicators.

- Provide mentoring and support for new managers and poorly performing managers

- Ensure that managers know how to address conflicts that are bought to their attention.

Employee Characteristics and the Social Environment
Risks in relation to employee characteristics and the social environment

Do you employ workers who may feel marginalised due to their age, sex, race, sexuality, disability, marital status, parenting status, pregnancy or religion?

(Yes/No/Not Sure)

Have your staff and managers undertaken diversity training to ensure that the needs of a diverse workforce are addressed?

(Yes/No/Not Sure)

Do you employ young workers including apprentices and trainees?

(Yes/No/Not Sure)

Do you have a male-dominated staff ratio or women employed in traditionally male areas of work?

(Yes/No/Not Sure)

Do you employ older workers who may be thinking of retiring soon?

(Yes/No/Not Sure)

Are there areas in the organisation where there are large amounts of sick leave taken, which are not in proportion to most departments?

(Yes/No/Not Sure)

Has the organisation had any workers compensation claims for psychological injury?

(Yes/No/Not Sure)

Do you have employees working in geographically isolated areas?

(Yes/No/Not Sure)

Are all your workers aware of their rights and responsibilities in relation to bullying?

(Yes/No/Not Sure)

Does the organisation carry out exit interviews with employees who are leaving the organisation?

(Yes/No/Not Sure)

If you answered YES or Not Sure to any of the questions in this section, you may need to do one or more of the following in order to control this risk:

- Ensure that all workers are employed and promoted on merit and according to a specific job description.
- Provide flexibility to reasonably accommodate the needs of different workers, such as those with disabilities, parenting obligations or religious needs.
- Develop a culture where diversity is respected and valued.
- Offer workers and management opportunities for professional and career development.
- Plan for the retirement of older workers by providing staged retirement options if possible.
- Offer new, young workers or vulnerable workers a buddy system to help them integrate into the workforce.
- Have a fair system set up where workers can seek assistance if they feel they are being treated unfairly.
- Ensure that workers in isolated areas are able to speak to anyone about any concerns they may have.
- Ensure that all workers are aware of their rights and responsibilities under your organisation's respectful behaviour policy

by disseminating the policy to them and providing regular training.

- Carry out exit interviews with all employees who leave the organisation and ask for feedback on organisational culture.
- Provide training in diversity, conflict management, communication and other skills for all workers.

Conducting a Climate Survey

A tailored staff climate survey is another workplace assessment tool that can help identify potential risks in different areas of the organisation. Once again it is not a stand-alone instrument. A survey such as the one included at the end of this chapter can provide information about how employees perceive their work environment, the style of management, and the level of conflict within a workplace. Climate surveys also have value in initiating discussions and provide an opportunity for staff to raise issues/problems. A workplace risk assessment using a climate survey is not a formal investigation. Rather these surveys are used to gain a broad understanding of the environment or subjective perceptions of the workplace culture, prior to deciding what interventions may need to be implemented.

Climate surveys are not standardised or validated psychometric instruments, and can be amended to ask certain questions, or find out the prevalence or degree of risks that have already been identified. They can be developed as an online tool, or can supplement informal interviews and other workplace assessment tools. They are useful in team meetings to initiate discussion about the workplace environment, and used as part of the consultation process when designing OH&S systems. Climate surveys are part of a wider diagnostic process used to gather information on the perceptions of employees and managers about workplace issues or psychological risks at the team level. Results can form a valuable foundation for subsequent team discussions and training sessions.

Following the completion of the climate survey, the assessor can go through the workers responses with them and ask more specific questions about individual items, gaining a more thorough perspective of their perceptions of the workplace climate.

Once risks are identified, strategies can be developed to address issues raised and in order to minimise the risk of inappropriate behaviours occurring in the workplace.

A systematic approach to assessing the risk and developing and implementing risk minimisation strategies is important. There is no point in identifying that no managers have been trained in relation to their responsibilities to prevent bullying, and then carrying out training only once. There is no point in identifying that the level of sick leave is very high in one area because of high levels of stress, if there is no intervention, or follow-up.

Other systematic methods of identifying potential risk can be through:

- exit interviews
- examination of patterns of sick leave, absenteeism and staff turnover in different departments
- review of workers' compensation claims
- review of contacts with staff by OH&S representatives or bullying and harassment contact officers
- regular staff surveys and risk audits.

Remember, there may come a time when you need to justify your approach to preventing and managing bullying, sexual harassment or discrimination in a courtroom — try this quick quiz.

Imagine you were in court today and had to answer these questions:

- What endeavours has your organisation undertaken to identify the level of risk for bullying, sexual harassment and illegal discrimination occurring?
- Are these endeavours documented?
- When did you last carry out a risk assessment?
- What methods did you use to assess the risks, and do you have a copy of the findings?
- Has your organisation developed a respectful behaviour policy and grievance procedures?
- When were they updated/reviewed?
- When was the last time your managers had training in their responsibilities in preventing, including bullying, sexual harassment and discrimination?
- What does your policy direct managers to do if an employee complains about bullying or sexual harassment and asks them to keep the complaint confidential?
- Is management training in this area mandatory? If not, why not?
- Has your CEO and board had training regarding their responsibilities in this area?
- How would you describe the behaviour of your CEO and senior staff?
- Do they model appropriate behaviour? If not, how have you tried to address it?
- Have all employees received recent training regarding their rights and responsibilities in this area?
- Have you documented who received training?
- Was this training mandatory?

Team Climate Survey

This climate survey is part of a workplace assessment to assess the presence and degree of possible psychological safety risks. This is not an investigation. Results are used to help develop strategies and approaches to reducing the risks identified. Please feel free to expand on any of your answers or add any further comments.

Department_____

Name
(optional)_____

Please circle the number that best corresponds with your experiences.

1	2	3	4	5
Disagree completely	Somewhat disagree	Neither agree or disagree	Somewhat agree	Completely agree

1. My job allows me to use my skills, knowledge and experience

    1   2   3   4   5

2. I have a clear understanding of my job role and responsibilities

    1   2   3   4   5

3. I have a clear understanding of the reporting relationships in relation to my job

    1   2   3   4   5

4. I feel competent in using the technology that is needed to perform my job

    1   2   3   4   5

5. I feel safe in my job

    1   2   3   4   5

6. I feel able to talk to my manager if I have a problem

| 1 2 3 4 5

7. My manager allows me to carry out my work and provides me with support if needed

| 1 2 3 4 5

8. My colleagues and I work well together as a team

| 1 2 3 4 5

9. I feel threatened by clients or customers when performing my job

| 1 2 3 4 5

10. I feel that I am picked on at work by others because of a personal characteristic
(name that characteristic _____)

| 1 2 3 4 5

11. I have regular discussions with my manager about my work and role

| 1 2 3 4 5

12. I feel respected during those discussions

| 1 2 3 4 5

13. My manager takes my suggestions into account when making decisions

| 1 2 3 4 5

14. My manager is a good role model

| 1 2 3 4 5

15. My colleagues are friendly towards me

| 1 2 3 4 5

16. The team I work in has clear goals and objectives

    1   2   3   4   5

17. I have had the training necessary to carry out my job well

    1   2   3   4   5

18. Practical jokes that are not funny are often carried out in this department

    1   2   3   4   5

19. I am often asked to carry out tasks which clearly fall outside my job description.

    1   2   3   4   5

20. I work in a supportive team

    1   2   3   4   5

21. I am scared of someone I work with.If so, please indicate why_____

    1   2   3   4   5

22. My manager is 'just one of the team', and leaves us to manage ourselves

    1   2   3   4   5

23. My manager is committed to providing a supportive work-place

    1   2   3   4   5

24. The team I work in is exemplified by high levels of conflict

    1   2   3   4   5

25. My workplace is split into 'us' and 'them'

    1   2   3   4   5

Bullying is defined as repeated, unreasonable behaviour toward a worker or a group of workers that potentially creates a risk to their health or safety.

Using the supplied definition, please state whether you have been bullied at work over the last six months?

a) No ☐   b) Yes, very rarely ☐

c) Yes, now and then ☐   d) Yes, several times ☐
per month

e) Yes, several times ☐   f) Yes, almost daily ☐
per week

Who bullied you? (You may tick more than one category)

Supervisor or line manager/s ☐
Senior manager/s ☐
Colleagues/s ☐
Subordinate/s ☐
Client/s, customer/s, student/s ☐

How many were bullied?

Only you ☐
Yourself and several other work colleagues ☐
Everyone in your workgroup ☐

Who did you report the bullying to?

No one ☐
My manager ☐
Human Resources ☐
If you didn't report it, why_____

Has the issue been resolved?

No ☐   Yes ☐

Have you observed or witnessed bullying taking place at your workplace over the last 6 months?

No, never ☐   Yes, but rarely ☐

Yes, now and then ☐   Yes, often ☐

Sexual harassment is defined as ANY behaviour or activities of a sexual nature that are unwelcomed.

Using the above definition, please state whether you have been sexually harassed at work over the last six months?

a) No	☐	b) Yes, very rarely	☐
c) Yes, now and then	☐	d) Yes, several times per month	☐
e) Yes, several times per week	☐	f) Yes, almost daily	☐

Endnote

1 Standards Australia. HB 205-2004, *OHS Risk Management Handbook, Standards Australia*, Sydney, NSW, Australia. (2004)..

PART 3

Implementing Measures to Control the Risks

CHAPTER 7

Developing a Policy and an Integrated Complaint Management System

Developing a Policy

Organisations need policies for a range of reasons: to comply with laws, respond to stakeholder concerns, change behaviour, provide direction or clarification to employees and influence workplace culture. A policy on respectful workplace behaviours provides employees, including managers, with directives that ensure behaviours meet the standards set by the organisation, and are consistent with current anti-discrimination, sexual harassment and workplace bullying (OH&S) laws. A policy is enforceable, which means that breaches of the policy may incur disciplinary action.

A respectful behaviour policy:

• Informs all employees about the standard of behaviour expected from them.

- Specifically defines inappropriate and unacceptable behaviours that are covered by the policy such as workplace bullying, sexual harassment and unlawful discrimination.
- Informs employees that the standard of behaviour outlined by the policy is enforceable.
- Identifies the legislation that makes sexual harassment, discrimination and workplace bullying unlawful.
- Informs employees that that legal action can be taken against them for sexually harassing, discriminating against or bullying a fellow employee (or customer), and informs them that they could also be exposing the organisation to legal action if they carry out bullying or harassing behaviours.
- Integrates with a complaints procedure that provides a range of options and a structure to address complaints of inappropriate behaviour, including bullying, sexual harassment and discrimination.

A respectful workplace behaviour policy that identifies bullying, sexual harassment and unlawful discrimination, and sets standards of respectful behaviour, is part of a risk management system. A respectful behaviour policy should be integrated with the organisations conflict and complaint management system.

Behaviours such as bullying, sexual harassment and discrimination are more likely to occur in an organisation without an up-to-date policy and complaint management system, or in an organisation with a policy that is buried in the intranet, or sits in the top cupboard gathering dust. Workplace conflicts are more likely to escalate into disputes when there are no systems or mechanisms in place for employees to constructively resolve issues early. For this reason an integrated conflict management system that links respectful behaviour policy with ways of having a range of grievances from low level

- Does your organisation have a policy that sets a standard of behaviour that you want all of your staff to adhere to?

- Does your policy identify workplace bullying, sexual harassment and unlawful discrimination as examples of specific kinds of disrespectful behaviour?

- Does your policy provide the names of contact officers who can provide support and advice to employees who feel they are being sexually harassed, bullied or discriminated against?

- Does your complaint management system set out in clear terms a range of complaint options for all employees?

- Has your policy been updated in relation to changes in legislation that cover bullying, discrimination or sexual harassment?

- Does your policy address changes in ICT so that all staff are aware of their responsibilities in regard to required standards of behaviour via communication technologies?

conflicts to formal allegations of bullying is an important control measure.

When developing a respectful behaviour policy it is important to consult with workers and OH&S representatives. It is recommended that a key person assume responsibility for the development, implementation and review of the policy and the integrated complaint management system. This is usually a senior HR consultant or a senior person responsible for OH&S within the organisation. This person does not work in isolation but reports back to the executive and senior management.

Likewise, it is critically important to discuss issues with key staff such as OH&S representatives, equal opportunity advisors, union representatives and senior managers to ensure that the policy meets the needs of the organisation as a whole. Issues that may need to be addressed include compliance with external agencies such as OH&S regulations, equal opportunity and anti-discrimination laws, employee enterprise agreements and industrial regulations.

The coverage and content of the policy, which may different between organisations, must be scoped and discussed. For example, some organisations have separate bullying and equal opportunity/anti-discrimination policies. Other organisations amalgamate bullying, sexual harassment and equal opportunity into one policy labelled 'Bullying and Harassment' or include directives regarding them in a respectful behaviour policy. Whatever form it may take, a policy should abide by the principles of best practice and standards. Standards Australia provide up-to-date best practice standards in a number of areas including dispute management systems[1].

Resources for implementing the key policy directives need to be readily available and training, financial, staffing and compliance implications need to be taken into account.

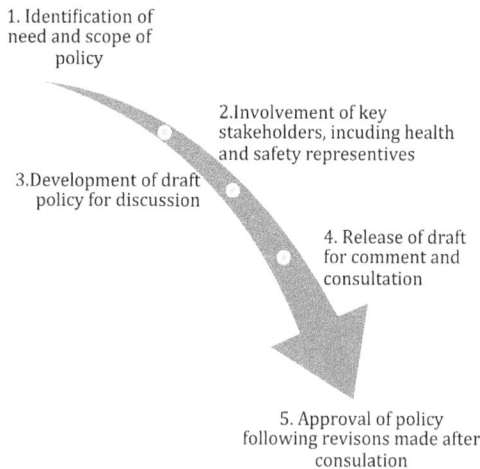

1. Identification of need and scope of policy

2.Involvement of key stakeholders, incuding health and safety representives

3.Development of draft policy for discussion

4. Release of draft for comment and consultation

5. Approval of policy following revisons made after consulation

Figure 7.1
Process to develop and implement new policy.

The path for final approval of the policy will vary across organisations. However, the policy should be approved by the chief executive or person ultimately responsible for ensuring that the organisation complies with industrial and safety standards in the workplace. (See Figure 7.1, for the process of creating the new policy.)

The new policy needs to be circulated to all staff (including managers and HR consultants) who should then be trained in relation to their rights and their specific responsibilities. There is little use of a policy if it just sits on a shelf or in an intranet and staff are not aware of their rights and responsibilities under the policy. There is little point having a policy if senior staff do not comply with the policy and model appropriate behaviour themselves.

While some organisations have separate policies and complaint procedures, most organisations incorporate complaint options as part of the same policy document. Having an integrated policy and complaints procedure means that employees do not have to go searching for separate documents, but can access both the policy and the conflict resolution options at the same time.

The following templates can be used when developing a respectful behaviour policy (incorporating directives regarding bullying, sexual harassment and unlawful discrimination) and integrated conflict management/complaint management system. These templates are provided as a guide only and I suggest that HR professionals take a customised approach to develop their own policy, based on the needs of their organisation, and the feedback from the consultation process.

When examining the templates, the column on the left provides helpful suggestions and recommendations, and the column on the right contains headings and specific sections that are necessary in a policy and complaints procedure.

Suggestions and guidance notes on developing your policy	Policy Framework
Ensure the policy has a clear title that informs the reader of its main purpose.	**TITLE** **Respectful Workplace Behaviour Policy** (Incorporating workplace bullying, sexual harassment and discrimination directives, as well as complaints procedures).
The next section of the policy addresses the purpose and context. Address how the organisation aims to meet the overall objectives set out in the purpose and context. Two examples are provided, but you, may want to provide more ways in which the organisation will meet its objectives.	**PURPOSE AND CONTEXT** This Respectful Workplace Behaviour policy ensures that: • all employees are afforded respect and fairness in all aspects of their employment, regardless of their personal characteristics or attributes • difference and diversity within the workforce is respected;employees are not depreciated because of their differences and characteristics • the benefits of employment are decided on merit, and not on irrelevant information • conflicts are resolved early, so as not to escalate into potentially harmful disputes. *Note: This policy covers all forms of unfair treatment and conflict including: discrimination, harassment, sexual harassment, bullying and victimisation; regardless of whether or not such unfair treatment is technically unlawful.* *Name of organisation* will do this by: • ensuring that all staff are aware of their rights and responsibilities in regard to workplace bullying, sexual harassment and discrimination • providing a fair, timely and effective conflict resolution procedure for employees and volunteers within name of organisation • *Add any other ways the organisation will implement the policy.*
You may want to highlight the specific business objectives of this policy, but not all policies have this section. Three examples are given. You may want to add more.	**The business objectives of this policy are:** • to promote a workplace that is respectful of all opinions • to promote a work environment that is productive, cooperative, constructive and healthy for all employees • to meet the legal legislative requirements of … • *Other business objectives you would like to add.*

Suggestions and guidance notes on developing your policy	Policy Framework
This section outlines the scope of this policy. Who does it apply to? Staff, students, clients, contractors, volunteers ... Are there limitations to the scope of the policy?	**SCOPE** This policy applies to... This policy also applies to ... For example: This policy does not preclude a person's right to lodge a complaint of unlawful discrimination, sexual harassment or bullying with the appropriate regulator or government agency (in Australia), such as: • the equal opportunity commission or anti-discrimination commission in each state • the Human Rights and Equal Opportunity Commission, Work Safe Australia, or state based OH&S regulators. ***Handy hint:*** *This policy does not only apply to employees while on work premises, but also at work related social events, conferences and locations outside the work site.*
This section addresses the legislative framework of the policy and complaints procedure. It can also include the Whistleblowers protection legislation, relevant industrial legalisation, enterprise agreements and state anti-discrimination and equal opportunity legislation.	**LEGISLATION** This policy is based on the legislative and ethical frameworks of the following Australian laws: • *Racial Discrimination Act* 1975 (Cth) • Racial Hatred Act 1995 (Cth) • *Sex Discrimination Act* 1984 (Cth) • *Australian Human Rights Commission Act* 1986 (Cth) • *Disability Discrimination Act* 1992 (Cth) • *Age Discrimination Act* 2004 (Cth) • *Work Health and Safety Act* 2011 (Cth) • OH&S laws of each state or territory relevant to the document • Any other relevant legislation you wish to add. ***Handy hint:*** *How about creating a hyperlink to the agency responsible for administering this legislation. Interested readers can find out more about the legislation if they want to.*
This section outlines the designated responsibilities of the senior staff that are involved in the implementation of aspects of this policy including training, collection of risks assessment data, responsibilities to ensure a healthy workplace, personal responsibilities to address inappropriate behaviour (even if it is not reported) and responsibilities to follow the directives in this policy.	**RESPONSIBILITIES** • **Director/CEO** Ensure that an equal employment opportunity and workplace bullying 'rights and responsibilities' program' are developed, implemented and annually reviewed. These programs will: • include training for all managers in regard to merit-based selection process

Suggestions and guidance notes on developing your policy	Policy Framework
Some of the key responsibilities of the Director/CEO might be delegated to other staff in the organisation	• include training for all managers in regard their responsibilities to prevent and address any potential discriminatory, harassing or bullying behaviours that may exist in operational areas;
	• develop, maintain and evaluate a systematic method of assessing the risk of workplace bullying, sexual harassment or discrimination occurring within the organisation and provide regular training to all personnel that are involved in this system, including contact officers, OH&SW representatives and HR consultants
	• effectively manage complaints of unfair treatment in accordance with the complaint handling options outlined in this policy
	• develop, maintain and use a systematic method to evaluate the way the organisation prevents and manages workplace bullying, sexual harassment and discrimination within the organisation.
The responsibilities of these other key personnel needs to be outlined	• **HR Manager** • **Managers** • **Employees** • **Workplace Contact Officers/OH&S Representatives**
In this section, you need to define all of the technical terms and keywords used in the policy. Some common technical terms are listed, but you may wish to add more. Your organisation needs to define all of these terms in its policy so all staff understand what they mean.	**DEFINITIONS** • **Bullying** (address what is bullying, what is NOT bullying) • **Conflict** • **Conflict coaching** • **Confidentiality** • **Cyberbullying** (provide examples of behaviours that might be cyberbullying) • **Employee Assistance Program** (may have electronic link to the organisation's EAP or contact phone numbers) • **Mediation** (see chapter 10 for outline of OH&S model of mediation) • **Natural justice** • **Place of employment** • **Respondent** • **Sexual harassment** (address what is not sexual harassment and examples of sexually harassing behaviours) • **Upwards bullying** • **Vexatious complaint** • **Victimisation** • **Workplace conferencing**

Small business need not have a large policy document like the one above, but might choose to have a one or two page document highlighting the organisations expected standards of behaviour. This one page document should define what bullying, unlawful discrimination and what sexual harassment is. It should make clear that the standard of behaviour expected by all employees, and that breaches of this standard of behaviour may result in disciplinary action. All employees should sign it as part of their workplace orientation, and each year of their employment. A copy of the expected standards of behaviour should be visibly displayed.

Integrating a Conflict Management System and Complaints Procedure

All organisations experience conflict. To progress, excel and develop, organisations may benefit from some healthy conflict and debate. Indeed the absence of healthy conflict and debate can indicate apathy or a fear of questioning established or entrenched working practices. However, conflict that alienates workers, makes them feel threatened and continues to escalate can easily become workplace bullying.

Escalated unhealthy conflicts can lead to entrenched disputes that undermine performance and team work. Unhealthy conflicts are those when one person or a group of people feel powerless, and feels disrespected by the other, who does not acknowledge their opinion, values or needs. Unhealthy conflicts cannot be ignored because of the potential for them to escalate into workplace bullying or harassment. Organisations cannot afford to address unhealthy conflicts in an ad hoc fashion, and they need to manage in a systemic and standardized manner. Organisations also need to have a number of different of processes to address the different types conflicts and disputes that can occur.

An integrated conflict management system[2] ensures that a systemic approach to preventing and resolving both low grade unhealthy conflicts, as well as more serious issues such as workplace bullying, harassment and discrimination. A conflict management system needs to be integrated with the organisations respectful behaviour policy, and includes a number of alternative processes to address conflicts, as well as options to address more serious breaches of the policy including bullying, sexual harassment and discrimination. This integrated conflict management system recognizes that conflict is a process, and therefore, different methods of resolution are required at different levels of conflict escalation. An integrated conflict management system also recognises that bullying is a serious occupational hazard. As such, it is not reasonable to expect targets to resolve bullying on their own. Indeed, expecting targets to utilise more informal approaches if they are being bullied, could place them in a more dangerous situation, and more formal processes may be more appropriate for complaints of bullying and harassment.

> **FEATURES OF AN INTEGRATED CONFLICT MANAGEMENT SYSTEM**
>
> 1. Addresses all types of conflicts including those between individual employees, between employees and managers, and conflicts within teams.
> 2. Addresses all levels of conflicts from low grade conflicts and disputes, to serious complaints of bullying, sexual harassment and discrimination that might require more formal forms of intervention.
> 3. Encourages resolution of conflicts at the lowest level through ADR process.
> 4. Provides multiple access points in order that disputes can be addressed in the most appropriate manner.
> 5. Provides ways in which all staff can increase their ability to manage conflicts effectively.
> 6. Provides necessary support for users of the system, including training for all users, including employees and managers.

Beginning with interest-based models of conflict management, the integrated conflict management system offers a number of individual, relationship and team based options to resolve conflicts. These early conflict management strategies are based on ADR process such as conflict coaching, team conferencing and mediation. These processes don't seek to blame or apportion guilt, but their primary purpose is to help the individuals involved resolve their conflict in a constructive manner. One of the features of an integrated conflict management system is the emphasis on early intervention and increasing conflict management competency. Therefore, conflict coaching is often encouraged at a number of levels. For example, conflict coaching is offered to employees and managers to increase their confidence and competence in managing and resolving a number of different types of conflicts ranging from interpersonal conflicts, to issues over performance management, team dynamics, or behavioural concerns. Conflict coaching is also useful prior to mediation to assist the parties prepare for the mediation itself. Conflict coaching can help both parties learn to communicate their perspective more effectively, manage their emotions and consider how to respond to the other person during the mediation[3]. Post mediation conflict coaching can also assist both parties to address any ongoing emotions or episodic clashes more constructively.

An integrated conflict management system also recognises that in some cases an ADR process might not be appropriate. For example, serious bullying or sexual harassment allegations may require third-party intervention and a formal investigation process. These more formal processes may also be followed with ADR practices on both an individual or team level. While formal processes are necessary, they are often insufficient when used on their own because they usually address only the allegation, not the source of the conflict itself. An OH&S approach to preventing bullying and harassment also addresses the source of the conflict following any formal intervention such as mediation or investigation.

The framework for the integrated conflict management system outlined is a guide only. As with the policy document, these templates are incomplete and are provided as a an outline only. By providing a guide only I aim to encourage HR professionals to consult with staff and take a customised approach to develop their own integrated conflict management system, based on the needs of their organisation.

Outline the process that supports your conflict management system. Outline the different options available to users of the system, and explain what each option involves.

The process of having a complaint conflict seriously and resolved through ADR process encouraged dialogue between the parties and an early resolution to conflicts. It provides a range of options that parties in a conflict can use to have their issues addressed. You may not want to utilise all of the options presented here, but they are worth discussing as part of your initial consultation process when you develop your own integrated conflict management system

Integrated conflict management system

Principles Supporting the Conflict Management System:
• This conflict management system supports the organisations Respectful Workplace Behaviour policy.
• This organisation takes will respond and act on any complaints of unresolved conflict, bullying, sexual harassment or unlawful discrimination;
• The complaint handling options will provide a fair and impartial process.
• The organisation will encourage an early conflict resolution/complaint resolution process that focuses on education and ADR processes.
• The organisation will implement disciplinary measures where the seriousness of the matter warrants it.
• The organisation will ensure there is no victimisation of the complainant or the respondent.
• The organisation will provide support to the all parties throughout the conflict/complaint resolution process.
• The management of complaints will adhere to the principles of fairness and natural justice for all parties involved in the complaint resolution process.

Step 1: ADR Conflict Resolution/Complaint Resolution Options
(a) Self-help *(what does this involve?)*
(b) Conflict coaching *(what does this involve?)*
(c) Self-help with assistance of conflict coach or contact officer *(what does this involve?)*
(d) Manager intervention/facilitated discussion with manager *(what does this involve?)*
(e) HR intervention/facilitated discussion with

HR consultant *(what does this involve?)*
(f) Workplace conferencing *(what does this involve?)*
(g) Mediation *(the OH&S model of mediation is recommended as part of an integrated conflict management system. This is outlined in chapter 10)*

While these initial processes are conciliatory options of conflict resolution, if the matter is serious (such as an assault or threats made to a person's psychological or physical safety or life), the complainant is to *(insert instruction to the complainant)*

Include instructions to managers in regard to their responsibilities to act on all complaints — whether they are verbal or written.

Managers who receive verbal or written complaints of bullying, sexual harassment or discrimination are to take them seriously and take appropriate action to address the concerns as soon as possible. Managers who receive complaints, either verbal or written, are to intervene, and follow up with both parties to ensure the alleged conduct is not still occurring. Complaints of bullying, sexual harassment and discrimination cannot be kept confidential and must be acted upon.

Managers who witness behaviours that are inappropriate, potentially discriminatory or a threat to health and safety, have a duty of care to address them even if a complaint has not been made by either party.

Formal Complaint Handling Processes

It is recommended that prior to a formal investigation, a mediation as outlined in chapter 10 is carried out. If the mediation does not resolve the issues (or if the issues are too serious to warrant a mediation), then a formal investigation can commence.

Prior to lodging a formal complaint, it is expected that the complainant has made a reasonable effort to address their concerns through the ADR options available.

1. The complainant must lodge a letter of complaint, marked 'Private and Confidential' to name of responsible officer, specifying the details of the allegations. An HR consultant or contact officer is able to assist the complainant to write a formal complaint letter if the complainant is unable to write it on their own. An HR officer or contact officer is NOT to write the letter of complaint for the complainant or on behalf of the complainant.

2. In order to investigate a complaint the investigator will need to know:

(a) The name of the person they are complaining about.
(b) What the specific behaviours the complainant is alleging occurred *(describe the specific behaviours)*.
(c) If there are, and who, are possible witnesses.

If the allegations are substantiated, then a recommendation for disciplinary action wil be made according to the organisations policy on disciplinary action.

Following an investigation it is also recommended that a workplace culture survey and workplace assessment are carried out in order to identify risk factors that may have contributed to the initial conflict, and escalation of the conflict.

Employees have a legal right to lodge a complaint with the appropriate external regulatory authority.

(d) Any other evidence or documentation to support the allegations.

3. Within *(specify how many)* working days of receiving the complaint *(name of responsible officer or his/her delegate)* will write to the complainant acknowledging the receipt of their complaint, and …

4. The *(responsible officer)* will inform the respondent that an investigation has begun in accordance with the formal investigation process.

5. Within *(specify how many)* working days of receiving the complaint, the *(responsible officer)* will write to the respondent stating:

• that a complaint against them has been received
• the specific alleged misconduct to be investigated
• that an investigation has begun in accordance with the formal investigation process
• that they will be interviewed to present their side of the story and are expected to attend all interviews

Independent Investigation Officer

Within *(specify how many)* working days of receiving notice from the delegated responsible person that a formal complaint is to be investigated, *(the delegated responsible person)* will contract and brief an external investigator to investigate the complaint;

Outcome of investigation

Within *(specify how many)* weeks of being contracted, the investigator will have carried out the investigation.

If this time period needs to be extended, the investigator will write to the ………….......
When the investigation is completed, the investigator will……………….................…

On receipt of the investigator's report, the ………….. will consider the findings and determine if further action is required.

When the complaint is finalised

The ……………. will ensure that all the investigation report and any other confidential records are stored in …………….................

All parties involved in the complaint/investigation process will be offered conflict coaching.

Any teams involved in systemic investigations may request workplace conferencing to address underlying conflicts or concerns that have contributed to, or stemmed from the investigation

Appealing an investigation into claims of bullying, sexual harassment or unlawful discrimination

Employees have a legal right, and may, at any time, choose to seek advice or to lodge a formal complaint with an external authority (in Australia), such as:

- State Equal Opportunity Commission/Anti-Discrimination Commission or
- Federal Human Rights Commission
- Work Safe Australia
- State OH&S regulatory authority

Endnote

1 Standards Australia 2004. *Australian Standard 4608-2004, Dispute Management Systems*, Standards Australia International Ltd, Sydney, NSW, Australia.

2 Costantino, C., & Merchant, C.S. (1996). *Designing conflict management systems: A guide to creating productive and healthy organisations.* San Francisco: CA: Josey-Bass.

3 Noble, C. (2012). *Conflict management coaching: The Cinergy model.* Toronto, Canada: Cinergy Coaching.

CHAPTER 8

Training Measures for Safer Work Environments

Types of Training

One of the important control measures that an organisation can implement is training their managers and employees in relation to their rights to work in a safe environment, and their responsibilities if they feel that others are behaving inappropriately. Organisations may also need to undertake cultural awareness or diversity training in order to address unintended systemic discrimination through stereotypes and prejudices that have the effect of marginalising specific groups of employees.

Diversity Training

Diversity training is about valuing differences. It is about treating people with respect and allowing all employees to be able to perform to their best level of ability without being constrained by preconceived ideas based on stereotypes.

Diversity training has a different emphasis to anti-discrimination or equal opportunity training because it covers a much wider framework than merely the legal requirements. Instead, diversity training also emphasises differences between individuals and the value and benefits that such difference brings to the organisation. It also addresses the problems of stereotyping groups of employees and the inherent prejudice that stereotypes brings.

Talking about, and with, the diverse groups within an organisation allows other views to be understood and accommodated by the dominant group. By having these discussions minority groups within the organisation gain a sense of being included rather than excluded. However, without taking the time to specifically notice and address this diversity, managers, HR professionals and employers are at risk of treating their workforce as homogenous, despite employees coming from a number of different cultures, religions, sexualities and other groups. Organisations with large groups of ethnically diverse employees may like to involve community leaders in the development and delivery of training, in order to bring a 'real-world' perspective. Specifically addressing and embracing diversity also passes on the message to employees that treating anyone badly because they belong to a minority group, will not be tolerated by the organisation.

Often in diversity training, participants raise issues that need to be fed back to a person in a position to do something about them. Employees should be kept informed about what action is being taken so that they know that the organisation is serious about managing diversity, and accommodating the needs of a diverse workforce.

Diversity Workshop

The learning objectives of a diversity workshop are to:

- Understand the legal framework underpinning workplace diversity
  - equal opportunity and anti-discrimination legislation
  - direct and indirect discrimination
- Understand the business case for diversity
  - employee recruitment, retention and satisfaction
  - customer service
  - organisational brand and reputation
- Understand what is meant by 'stereotypes' and 'prejudice' and how these constructs can negatively impact on groups of people in a diverse workforce
- Develop ways of building flexibility into the workplace to accommodate the needs of a diverse workforce.

Depending on the makeup of the workforce, other learning objectives might focus on understanding perceptions or problems faced by employees from certain ethnic groups. It may be appropriate to identify community members or employees who are interested in assisting in the development of the program and use their experiences to generate examples and exercises.

Managers may need specific learning objectives related to recruitment, performance management and challenges in managing a diverse workforce. These learning objectives are met through interactive discussions, small group activities and presentations from key community leaders or representatives.

Table 8.1 provides examples of ideas on how to accommodate some needs identified by different groups within a large organisation. These needs and suggestions for embracing diversity were added to over several training sessions held with different departments within the organisation. They were then feedback to HR. Employees received regular updates about actions that were being taken in relation to some of the suggestions

Table 8.1

Meeting the Needs of a Diverse Workforce

Identified Group	Suggested Ways of Meeting Needs
Religious needs	Prayer room Flexible working arrangements for those who observe the Sabbath on a Saturday Visit local mosque for an educational tour Halal food in the cafeteria
Parenting needs	Flexible hours to meet parenting requirements Offer subsidy for child care at local child care centre Family friendly work functions
Age Older workers	Planned reduction in hours for those that want to work part time prior to retiring Pre-retirement seminars
Younger workers (graduates/trainees and apprentices)	Mentoring system for younger workers
Employees with English as a second language	Assistance in English language classes Interpreter offered for important discussions
Workers with a disability	Identify needs of individual workers and examine how these can be accommodated Mental health first aid course
Indigenous workers	Indigenous mentor Support group
Women	Mentoring schemes Flexibility in returning to work following maternity leave
Sexual diversity	Mentoring schemes Meeting area for gay, lesbian, bisexual, transgender and intersex employees

Another important aspect of managing diversity is to address the concept of stereotypes and how this contributes to prejudice and discrimination and the impact on people in the workforce (see Table 8.2). In one activity that I carry out, workshop participants are provided with definitions of 'stereotype' and 'prejudice' and then in small groups discuss and feed back to the larger group, inherit problems caused by these constructs.

Table 8.2

The Impact of Stereotypes and Prejudices

Stereotypes	Weakness	Impact
A series of widely held generalisations about a group or class of peoplethat are based on some prior assumptions	Ridged Simplistic One dimensional view of people	Pigeon hole people / groups Negative view of people in that group Sometimes unrealistic positive view of people in that group Contribute to prejudice Simplistic and inaccurate assumptions made about individuals Contributes to unfair behaviours as the unique talents of individuals are not catered for or recognised

Prejudice	Weakness	Impact
An negative attitude that has been formed because of inaccurate or incomplete information, or stereotypes	Inaccurate judgments that contribute to erroneous decisions being made Negative assumptions are made about individuals based on stereotypes Individual attributes, strengths and personality characteristics are ignored in favour of inaccurate attributes based on stereotypes	Discrimination Poor educational and career prospects Poor given opportunities to advance Can contribute to inappropriate or negative behaviours from others Prejudice prevents some people in stereotyped groups from entering or succeeding in various activities or occupations Can contribute to some groups of people being subjugated and dominated by a more powerful group Injustice on a personal, societal and global scale

Rights and Responsibilities

Training in 'rights and responsibilities' is an essential part of developing a workplace that is free of bullying and harassment. Contact officers and OH&S representatives also need to have regular training in relation to their specific responsibilities in preventing bullying and harassment.

A training session can easily become 'death by PowerPoint' if it is delivered as a lecture, focusing on the facts and 'telling participants what to do'. People learn more effectively if an interactive approach is used, and if they feel involved in the learning process. Talking about bullying, sexual harassment and discrimination can be an exciting topic. Talking about real cases brings the subject alive, as workshop participants relate to the experience of targets. Employees all have their own stories about bullying, and these examples can be used to explore what bullying is, and is not, and what their options are to address the behaviour. Managers too, have stories about how they have had to deal with poor behaviours and allegations of bullying or harassment. Training should be part of the ongoing risk management process. Feedback from employees and managers in regard to risks present in their work area, or behaviours that may be occurring, should inform the OH&S strategy. Because the OH&S approach to preventing bullying is a dynamic process, there should be continual consultation with employees, managers and different stakeholders to improve the system and prevent bullying from occurring. Training is a opportunity to consult with stakeholders before, during and after training programs. Often during training sessions participants will talk about inappropriate behaviours that they have witnessed. In other sessions participants have complained that while base-grade employees are expected to behave respectfully, senior management appear to continually bully and behave as they wish. This is important information in relation to risk assessment and management.

In training groups where there are a range of management levels, more senior or experienced managers can pass on important tips to the junior managers, and the experiences and knowledge of the participants can be both interesting and valuable learning tools. Groups of no more than 12 to 15 participants help keep the training interactive. Groups that are too big do not interact very well, and make it difficult for trainers to coordinate activities and undertake small group exercises.

I often start 'rights and responsibilities' training with an 'ice-breaker' that is relevant to the group. The icebreakers need to be relevant to the group participants. You wouldn't use the same ice-breaker activity for the senior management team that you might use for the employees. You might use a different type of icebreaker with a group of blue-collar workers than you would with a group of professional white-collar employees.

'Where Do You Stand' Icebreaker

What you need: Three A4 cards with 'AGREE', 'DISAGREE' and 'NEUTRAL' printed on them. The 'AGREE' card is placed at one end of the room, the 'DISAGREE' card at the other end and the 'NEUTRAL' card in the middle of the room.

The trainer asks group participants to stand up and move together to the middle of the room. A provocative statement such as *'The workplace has become much too politically correct'* is read to the group, and participants are asked to move to the area of the room that reflects whether they agree, disagree or feel neutral in response to the statement. The trainer then asks various participants why they agree, disagree or are neutral. Their responses introduce the topic of bullying, sexual harass-ment and discrimination to participants in an interactive and fun way. Follow-up questions can further stimulate thought and challenge participants. Often the participants in the group chal-lenge each other. This type of activity also promotes an interac-tive training environment in which each participant can make a valuable contribution.

Provocative statements can be positioned within more serious assertions. At times, light-hearted statements regarding the local football team or sporting identity in the news might help break the ice and encourage interaction and banter among participants who are initially reluctant to participate. Some questions that can be used in a 'where do you stand' warm-up exercise are shown in the following example.

EXAMPLE QUESTIONS — WHERE DO YOU STAND? (AGREE, DISAGREE OR NEUTRAL

1. The workplace has become much too politically correct. Follow-up questions could be:
   - In what way?/What do you mean?
   - What is wrong with political correctness?/Where do you draw the line?
   - What is the difference between political correctness and respect?

2. People who feel they are being bullied are just oversensitive. Follow-up questions could be:
   - Where do you draw the line? /When does a joke become bullying?
   - Can bullying be unintentional?
   - How do you know if someone doesn't like what you are saying or how you are behaving?
   - Why might they not say anything?
   - What is the worst thing that can happen to someone who is bullied? (The answers can be used to draw attention to the effects of bullying.)

3. People aren't responsible for their own actions these days. Follow-up questions could be:
   - Do laws take away personal responsibility for a safe workplace?
   - What are your personal responsibilities for a safe workplace?
   - What do we mean by a safe workplace?

4. You can't teach old dogs new tricks.(This statement can be used to introduce the concept of stereotypes and discrimination.)

5. All bullies are psychopaths.

6. All these sexual harassment laws and safety laws have taken the fun out of the workplace.

When conducting training for managers and employees, it is worthwhile working through the advantages and disadvantages in each of the complaint options in the organisation's policy and complaints procedure. It is important that the trainer fully understand these options themselves. There is no point in the trainer talking about the advantages and disadvantages of conflict coaching or mediation, if they do not have a good understanding of these concepts.

Every option has its benefits and challenges. However in general, the more formal the complaint is, the more adversarial and legalistic it becomes and the less control the individuals involved will have over the outcome and process. A useful exercise is to divide participants into five groups: (1) self-help, (2) manager intervention, (3) mediation, (4) formal internal investigation, and (5) external complaint to a regulatory body. Each group then discusses the advantages and disadvantage of each complaint handling option and writes them down on paper. They then report back to the whole group, and the group discusses the advantages and possible disadvantages of a particular option (see Table 8.3). This provides further opportunity for the trainer to expand on any of the points made or correct any misconceptions about what is involved in the various complaint options. Managers can also discuss the advantages and disadvantages of each option from an organisational perspective.

One of the most common pieces of feedback I receive is that the participants enjoyed and learned from the cases and stories discussed. All of these case studies are relevant learning opportunities and we can learn from the mistakes of others.

A number of cases that have been to court are discussed in this book, but there are a number of sexual harassment or discrimination cases that have been conciliated or mediated through state, territory and national anti-discrimination/equal opportunity agencies. As they have been through conciliation, specific details have been changed to preserve the anonymity of

Table 8.3

Approaches, Advantages and Possible Disadvantages of Conflict and Resolution Training

Approaches	Advantages	Possible Disadvantages
1. Self-Help (i.e., talking to the other party yourself)	• Useful for minor conflicts • Empowering to individuals • Can clear up misunderstandings and maintain the relationship	• Possibility of escalation or victimisation • Organisation not aware of behaviours occurring • No examination of systemic issues that contributed to the poor behaviour and so these may continue to contribute to ongoing conflict and escalation of the behaviour • An angry target may retaliate and then be further victimised • A target may not have the necessary skills to approach and discuss their concerns with the other person
2. Manager intervention	• Keeps the issue between the individuals involved • Encourages individuals to take responsibility with a third party monitoring future behaviour • Encourages managers to take responsibility and be seen to be acting to stop inappropriate behaviours Nips the problem in the bud before it escalates further • Can monitor the environment for further poor behaviours and intervene • Has the option to implement team-based interventions to address issues that may have contributed to the poor behaviours.	• Manager may have poor conflict management skills/training • Behaviour may be driven 'underground' • Because of the workplace environment there may be no examination of systemic issues that contributed to the poor behaviour • Behaviour may be justified as 'normal' and not challenged or misdiagnosed as a conflict or 'personality clash' • Management style may be supporting a bullying culture.
3. Mediation	• Empowers both parties to resolve the dispute in a way that they both have a say in the outcome • Can accommodate the needs of both parties, as it is a flexible process • Can discuss issues that contributed to the behaviour	• Unless addressed by the mediator, mediation has the potential to hide poor behaviours from further scrutiny by the organisation • Unless resolution agreements are followed up, there is no accountability, and they may not be adhered to

CONTINUE OVER

Table 8.3 (Continued)

Approaches, Advantages and Possible Disadvantages of Conflict and Resolution Training

Approaches	Advantages	Possible Disadvantages
	• Contributes to better communication between the parties, so they can understand each other's perspective • Aims to resolve the issues and is not about blaming or implying guilt • No determination of facts • Offers a range of options to resolve the dispute • Examines perceptions, not positions • Gives both parties control over the process • Can address the systemic issues if an OH&S mediation framework is used (see chapter 11) • Settlement agreements may be followed up by the relevant manager or HR to ensure appropriate behaviour in the future	• Unless the OH&S model of mediation (see chapter 10) is utilised background factors or risk factors that contributed to the behaviour might not be identified. This means there is potential for further conflict and poor behaviours in the future • Bullying where one party has suffered significant injury and the other party is continuing to exhibit threatening or intimidating behaviour is not appropriate for mediation.
4. Formal internal investigation	• The complaint may or may not be substantiated, resulting in a finding of guilty or not guilty based on the balance of probabilities • Disciplinary action may be taken against the perpetrator if complaint substantiated • Organisation is in control of the process.	• Respondent has no control over the process or findings • Complainant has less control over the process than they have in mediation and no control over the findings • An investigation relies on establishing facts that are often difficult to prove • The complainant may not find out what disciplinary action has been taken against the perpetrator if the complaint is substantiated. This may make them disappointed • Investigation by its nature is an adversarial process. There is a winner and a loser

CONTINUE OVER

Table 8.3 (CONTINUED)

Approaches, Advantages and Possible Disadvantages of Conflict and Resolution Training

Approaches	Advantages	Possible Disadvantages
		• More people become involved, as witnesses are called • There is a potential to split teams and cause wider conflict • The focus is on individual behaviours, not on organisational antecedents • Difficult to substantiate as much of bullying is covert and subjective (e.g., the behaviour might be unreasonable and threatening, but might not meet the definition of bullying)
5. External complaint v a regulatory authority	• External process and investigation, so no interference from an organisation trying to protect its own interests • For sexual harassment and discrimination complaints mediation or conciliation with a trained mediator/ conciliator specialising in the area is usually the first process in an external complaint • Most cases that go through the court system are open to public scrutiny	• Need to adhere to specified time limits • Will only examine whether the complaint meets the legal definition of bullying, sexual harassment, etc. (see *McKibbibin v the Office of the Public Trustee*)[2] May not find in favour of the complainant (see *Sluggett v Commonwealth of Australia*[3] • The organisation has no control over the process • By the time a case goes to court, the likelihood of a number of employee WorkCover claims for stress-related illness has increased substantially. This may lead to an increase in insurance premiums • A long process that may take years to get to court. Most cases settle out of court following mediation • Lawyers involved, which increases the costs to the organisation

CONTINUE OVER

Table 8.3 (Continued)

Approaches, Advantages and Possible Disadvantages of Conflict and Resolution Training

Approaches	Advantages	Possible Disadvantages
		• There is a greater likelihood of negative publicity for the organisation
		• Proceedings can be very adversarial and hostile, contributing to extra stress for all parties, including witnesses, HR professionals who are called to give evidence and managers and chief executives who are responsible for preventing and stopping workplace hazards

the parties, but they provide a good example of the types of issues that have gone wrong. For example, the AHRC web site (www.hreoc.gov.au) describes a large number of conciliated cases of sexual harassment, race, sex, age and disability discrimination in the workplace. Similar cases studies can be found in most of the state and territory anti-discrimination or equal opportunity agency websites. Legal cases can be found through the Australasian Legal Information Institute (www.austlii.edu.au). Often court decisions contain very important messages that can be used in training to inform participants of their rights and responsibilities regarding bullying, sexual harassment or discrimination. They also illustrate the organisational risk factors that have contributed to the behaviour. Some cases also illustrate that not every case of bullying, sexual harassment or discrimination that is taken to court is substantiated.

As anti-discrimination and equal opportunity laws are different for each state and territory, it is important that trainers be aware of what attributes or 'grounds' of discrimination are covered.

Training for Managers

The training program agenda below outlines the objectives in relation to the responsibilities of managers in preventing and addressing workplace discrimination, sexual harassment and bullying. It takes an OH&S perspective.

The learning objectives of this training program are to:

- Review anti-discrimination, sexual harassment and OH&S laws as they pertain to psychological health and safety in the workplace

- Understand how to take a risk management approach to assess and address workplace bullying, sexual harassment and unlawful discrimination from within an OH&S framework, including:
  - assessing potential risks within your organisation/department
  - identifying risks
  - mitigating or controlling risks

- Understand the personal responsibilities of a manager in relation to preventing workplace bullying, discrimination and sexual harassment

- Understand the personal responsibilities of a manager in relation to managing verbal and written complaints, and what to do if witness to behaviours that potentially may be workplace bullying, discrimination or sexual harassment

- Understand the risks of 'off-site work functions' in contributing to sexual harassment, discrimination and bullying complaints

- Understand what is meant by the term 'vicarious liability' and what managers' responsibilities are in relation to mitigating that liability

- Understand the advantages and disadvantages of each of the complaint handing options available to staff in your organisation's 'fair treatment in the workplace' (bullying, discrimination and harassment)' policy and complaints procedure

- Understand how your managerial 'duty of care' responsibilities can affect 'confidentiality' and the way you manage complaints
- Understand the risks involved with mismanagement of informal and formal complaints of bullying, discrimination and sexual harassment.

These learning objectives are met though PowerPoint presentations, interactive group discussions using video/DVD scenarios, and discussion of state and national legal cases. Participants complete a risk management tool, and subsequent discussion about responses highlights potential risks within their different departments. Ways in which these risks can be managed or controlled are discussed as a group.

Some of the common dilemmas bought up by managers in training sessions a examined below.

'I was asked to keep the complainant confidential, so I couldn't do anything about it'.

Because of their duty of care to prevent and address potential psychological hazards (caused by bullying discriminatory or sexual harassment behaviour), there is no such thing as 'absolute confidentiality'. Confidentiality means that only the people who are directly involved with the complaint are to be spoken to about the matter. It does not mean that the manager is not to speak to anyone about the complaint. As managers have a duty of care to staff, they may not be able to keep a complaint of potential bullying, sexual harassment or discrimination absolutely confidential. A manager *must* act in some way to prevent workplace hazards including psychological hazards from occurring. What they do, and the degree to which they take action, is depend on how they assess the risk. In the first instance a manager may act by following up with the employee and asking them if the alleged behaviour is still occurring (not forgetting to document that they have followed up), and if the behaviour is still occurring they can then discuss with the employee what further steps can be taken to address the problem.

'I can't investigate the allegations until I receive a written formal complaint'
This is incorrect. Managers are obliged to address all verbal and written complaints of discrimination, sexual harassment and bullying. Even prior to a complaint, if a manager witness potentially discriminatory, harassing or bullying behaviour they need to act. A number of organisations have policies and complaints procedures that instruct complainants to complete a written complaint before action can be taken. Some even direct complainants to complete and submit specific forms, and advise that complaints will not be accepted unless they are written down. However, in the case of *McKibbin v the Office of the Public Trustee*, Judge Rice made the following statement:[4]

> It is not enough to wait for a complaint before appropriate action needs to be taken by managers/employers. An employer's obligation to prevent discrimination, harassment and victimisation does not begin at the time that a formal complaint (e.g., a written note from, or documentation provided by, a complainant to an employer, or a written note from, or documentation provided by, an employee or manager witnessing the behaviour) is made. Certainly, if at the time a formal complaint is made, it is the first time that the employer is made aware that potentially discriminatory, harassing or victimising behaviour has occurred, and the employer takes appropriate and immediate action in response including reasonable steps to prevent contravention of the Act, the employer is more likely to have met the requisite statutory standard to avoid vicarious liability. However, if an employer is made aware informally of potentially discriminatory, harassing or victimising behaviour (e.g., observations of staff verbally conveyed to management, management observing relevant behaviour and so on) prior to a formal complaint

being made, and the employer takes no action until the formal complaint is made, the fact the employer takes appropriate and commensurate action in response would not be sufficient to avoid its being found vicariously liable.

This means that a manager's responsibility to prevent and stop discrimination, sexual harassment and bullying does not begin at the time that a formal complaint is lodged. Even if a complainant does not lodge a formal written complainant, a manager or employer is obliged to act on verbal complaints. In order to conduct a formal investigation, a manager or HR consultant who is made aware of potential discrimination, bullying or harassing behaviour may need to sit down with the complainant and assist them in writing down exactly what occurred in order for it to be formally investigated. A complainant may be so upset and intimidated by the behaviour that they are being subjected to that they are unable to formulate a coherent statement, or formal complaint on their own. The message here is don't wait until a formal complaint is lodged before you act. Managers are obliged to act on verbal as well as written complaints. If a manager knows that there is potential bullying, discrimination or sexual harassment occurring and does nothing about it until a formal written complaint is lodged, the fact that they then acted swiftly and appropriately does not mean they would not be found responsible for the behaviour occurring.

Training for Employees

A training program for employees highlights the rights of every employee to work in a safe and respectful environment and addresses employee responsibilities to treat peers and managers with professional respect. The training program outlines what is meant by 'discrimination', 'sexual harassment' and 'workplace bullying' and the effects of these behaviours on both the target and the organisation. It also outlines the options available to all employees under the organisation's 'respectful behaviour in the workplace' policy (incorporating workplace bullying, sexual harassment and discrimination policy and complaints procedures), and the advantages and disadvantages of each complaint option. The training program highlights the importance of witness coming forward and speaking up against potentially harmful behaviours.

It is important that employees know what bullying is, and what it is not. The research indicates that many employees use the term 'bullying' to describe a number of behaviours that are not bullying[5] including conflicts, reasonable although unpopular management behaviours and decisions, and unpopular changes that occur in organisations. Therefore, it is important for employees to be made aware that while many workplace decisions, management actions and behaviours are unpopular, they are not bullying.

The learning objectives of this session are:

- For employees to be aware of their 'rights' in relation to working in a respectful environment

- To understand their 'Responsibilities' in relation to treating their colleagues, managers and customers with professional respect

- To understand what is meant by 'discrimination' and 'sexual harassment'

- To understand what 'workplace bullying' is, and what bullying is not, including the difference between bullying and reasonable managerial direction

- To understand the impact of discrimination, sexual harassment and workplace bullying on individuals and organisations

- To understand the importance of witness speaking out in support those that they see being treated disrespectfully and unfairly.

- To understand what their options are under their organisation's 'Fair Treatment in the Workplace' policy and complaints procedures

- To understand the advantages and disadvantages of each option under the organisation's complaints procedures.

Again, this training is accompanied by activities and discussion to enhance learning. Small group activities will engage participants and provide opportunities to raise specific issues, and to discuss them in an interactive group. I use the following two activities with employee groups. These outlined activities include examples from a specific training session.

Activity 1: What Is Bullying/What Is Not Bullying?

Firstly, I divide the participants into two groups and ask participants in one group to write the different types of bullying behaviours they can think of on a large sheet of paper. If it is a large group, I might ask a third group to write down types of behaviour that can be sexual harassment or discrimination.

The other group is instructed to write a list of reasonable management actions, and behaviours that are not bullying (or discrimination or sexual harassment).

The completed lists are displayed where everyone can see them, and a spokesperson for each group presents each list, and with guidance from the trainer, leads the discussion about what bullying is, and what it is not.

Table 8.4 provides examples of some of the ideas presented by a recent group on what was bullying and what was reasonable management. These ideas were discussed more fully with all of the participants as they were being presented by the group. Table 8.4 shows cyberbullying was discussed at some length, and this raised the topic of the work/home divide. Some employees in this particular group worked from home, and employees often attended meetings at restaurants or licensed venues where the atmosphere was more relaxed. Some sites organised 'after work' drinks, conferences were held away from the workplace, often requiring overnight stays, and many employees spent considerable time away from the office. It was, therefore, important to emphasise that if poor behaviours (such as bullying, sexual harassment or discrimination) occur in any of those situations away from the 'workplace', they may still be considered work related, and the perpetrators may be held personally responsible for their poor behaviour and the organisation vicariously responsible.

Table 8.4

Activity 1— Perceived Bullying Behaviours and Reasonable Behaviours

Bullying Behaviours	Reasonable Behaviours
• Yelling, throwing things	• Monitoring performance to ensure a consistent reasonable standard is kept
• Purposely giving someone an unmanageable workload and the worst shifts	• Counselling me/telling me off if I make a mistake
• Picking on a colleague or on a manager and treating them badly	
• Always asking one person to do overtime at short notice, and not asking anyone else	• Not giving me a promotion for justifiable reason
• Playing practical jokes on someone that they don't like or find offensive	• Asking me to work overtime because we are being audited and need to catch up on specific work, (and sharing the load)
• Not letting someone have holidays when they want but letting others have their preferred holidays	• Having a shared joke with a friend (as long as the joke doesn't put anyone down or is not potentially offensive)
• Conducting initiation practices that are harmful or offensive (i.e., locking the apprentice in the broom cupboard)	• Celebrating the end of someone's probation or apprenticeship in a fun and respectful way
• Sending intimidating or rude text messages about someone	• Asking a work friend out for a coffee
• Saying bad things about someone on Facebook (even if this is done outside of work)	• Giving a mutual friend a hug is not harassment if it is welcomed
• Continually asking someone out when they have said no might be viewed as sexual harassment	• Asking staff for their opinions but choosing not to act on them
	• Setting reasonable standards of work
• Teasing someone or treating them badly because of their race, religion, sex, disability, sexuality or other characteristics may be both bullying and unlawful discrimination	• Terminating a staff member's employment for justifiable reasons after following necessary dismissal guidelines
• Constantly refusing to carry out work that you have been asked to do purposely to get your manager into trouble	• Providing some employees with flexibility to accommodate their specific needs (i.e., disability, child care needs) is not bullying the others who are not given the same level of flexibility
• Intimidating your manager through your body language, behaviour or by what you say to them or about them	• Telling someone to re-do a report that is not up to standard, if it is actually not up to standard.

Activity 2: The Consequences of Workplace Bullying and Harassment

Another group activity that I often ask participants to carry out spearheads a discussion on the potential consequences of bullying, sexual harassment and discrimination. Again, participants are divided into two groups, with one group writing down on a large sheet of paper the potential consequences of bullying and harassment for individuals, and the other group writing down the potential consequences for the organisation. A spokesperson from each group leads the discussion and the all group participants are encouraged to expand on each point and discuss further. In one workshop that I conducted, participants identified consequences (see Table 8.5), which we then expanded on as a group.

Table 8.5

Activity 2 — Identified Individual and Organisational Consequences

Individual Consequences	Organisational Consequences

• Depression, anxiety, other mental health issues — has led to suicide in some cases
• Increased physical health problems
• Poor sleep
  – can lead to mistakes being made at work
  – can lead to physical accidents at work as the target is anxious, tired and not concentrating
• Increased alcohol/drugs (prescribed and not prescribed)
• Poor confidence and self-esteem
• Poor work performance because they are so anxious; can make bullying worse, as the bully can focus on this
• Increased anger
  – can lead to retaliation and revenge
  – can affect family relationships
  – can affect other individuals in the area and witnesses to the bullying
	• Poor productivity
	• Increased sick leave
	• Increase in staff turnover
	• Increased WorkCover/legal claims and costs
	• Poor publicity if legal claims (e.g., sexual harassment and bullying cases are often in the media)
	• Increase in accidents because victim is nervous/anxious
	• Poor reputation of organisation
	• Loss of staff who leave due to poor atmosphere/culture
	• 'Splitting' of teams, as some people support the bully and others support the target
	• No innovation, as staff 'keep their head down' to avoid being bullied

Training for Contact Officers

Contact officers are an important part of an organisation's complaint management system. They are specifically trained to provide information to employees about their options in resolving complaints of conflict, bullying, sexual harassment or discrimination. This role also requires the contact officer to:

- assist a highly emotional employee to calm down and talk rationally about their concerns

- provide the employee with the organisation's complaint options and talk through the advantages and disadvantages of each option

- accompany, as a support person, the aggrieved employee to any meetings, mediations or to speak with their manager

- refer the aggrieved employee to counselling or other support services such as the organisation's EAP

- maintain statistical information about each enquiry/contact, and passes this information on to the HR department.

Because workplace bullying is viewed as an OH&S hazard, some organisations assign and train their OH&S representatives with the dual role of being a contact officer. It is recommended that the group of employees carrying out the role of contact officers reflect the diversity of their organisation and are *not* in a management role. This is because managers have a legal obligation to follow up and intervene in any potential discriminating, harassing or bullying behaviour. If a manager hears about any behaviour that has the potential to cause harm to another employee, they cannot keep that information confidential (as can a contact officer; see the following outline of the responsibilities and role of a contact officer at an initial interview). They have a duty of care to act, and prevent harm from occurring. An employee cannot go to a manager on a confidential basis and tell them they are being sexually harassed or bullied, and expect the manager not to take some form of action.

Table 8.6

Initial interview with the Contact Officer

The Initial Interview	Actions Required

• Opening statement
  – Outline your role
  – What you can and cannot do
  – Limits of confidentiality
• What are their concerns?
  – Listen with your EAR (empathy, attention and respect)
  – Summarise their concerns—anything else?
  – Check safety?
• What have they tried to do to resolve the problem?
  – What would they like to do?
  – Explore options—pros and cons
  – Any other options?
  – What will happen if they do nothing?
  – Who else can help?
  – Can they talk to their manager or HR?
• Next step
  – Provide copy of policy and complaint options
  – Do they want to meet again?
  – Complete 'enquirer interaction' form'
	• Act as the first port of call and provide information to an enquirer with a concern about workplace conflict, discrimination sexual harassment or bullying.
	• Actively listen to the enquirer.
	• Discuss options available to them and work through the advantages and disadvantages of each option.
	• Be present for support if the enquirer want to talk to the person they are in conflict with.
	• Assist an enquirer to find a way that will resolve the conflict without inflaming the situation.
	• Refer the enquirer to someone who may be able to actively intervene (as this is not the role of the contact officer)
	• Complete 'enquirer interaction' Form and keep issue confidential unless safety is compromised.
	• If safety is a concern, talk to designated person from HR

The contact officer can provide support to the enquirer if they want to talk to the person with whom they are in conflict. However, it is *not* the role of the contact officer to intervene, mediate, investigate or try to resolve the issues.

Some experienced or senior contact officers may have extra training in conflict coaching. Conflict coaching is a specific process that teaches skills that help individuals respond to high conflict situations in a way that is more likely to resolve the issue. Conflict coaching assists the participant to view the conflict from a number of different perspectives and helps to map out the advantages and disadvantages of different solutions to address the problem. Conflict coaching can also help participants examine how their own thoughts, judgements and actions may have contributed to the conflict. Conflict coaching is highly recommended for both parties prior to mediation as it assists in helping both parties view the issues from the others perspective, and examine the advantages and disadvantages of resolving the conflict from a number of different perspectives, in a number of different ways. Conflict coaching might help a target of workplace bullying realise that here is nothing that they can do to stop the behaviour, and their best option is to submit a formal complaint.

A contact officer also models appropriate workplace conduct. Just as an OH&S representative has the working knowledge to point out physical (and psychological) risks in the work environment, a contact officer is able to draw attention to behaviour that may be unlawful discrimination, sexually inappropriate or interpreted as bullying. A contact officer may choose to provide a short commentary on their role, or on the organisation's respectful behaviour policy at staff meetings or lunchtime seminars.

In most circumstances, the interaction between the contact officer and the enquirer is confidential. The contact officer only passes on statistical information to the HR department about their interaction with the enquirer. The exception to this is if the contact officer has seen the enquirer on a number of occasions and they believe the behaviour described is escalating, and the enquirer may be at risk of injury (either physical or psychological) because of the behaviour they are being subjected to. The contact officer is then to discuss their concerns with a designated person from the HR department.

Desirable Skills and Competencies
Leadership
A contact officer should have strong leadership qualities, which include:

- the ability to be proactive in order to prevent occurrences of inappropriate workplace behaviours such as sexual harassment, bullying or unlawful discrimination

- the ability to model attitudes and behaviours that are respectful and inclusive of diversity
- the ability to help others understand the organisation's approach is to show respectful behaviours towards all employees irrespective of their personal characteristics, background or hierarchical position in the organisation.
- the ability to raise awareness about bullying, sexual harassment and discrimination in their area.
- the ability to raise awareness about what behaviours are *not* bullying, so that the label of bullying is not applied to arbitrary, unpopular behaviours.

Communication

Communication skills are of paramount importance in the role of contact officer. A contact officer should have demonstrated abilities to:

- listen effectively to employees and managers from all facets of an organisation.
- communicate clearly and confidently to all levels of the workforce including senior management.
- clearly explain ideas and facts in a non-judgemental manner.
- effectively manage situations that deal with strong emotions including anger and distress.
- clearly identify and articulate the nature of the problems being presented.
- clearly communicate the range of options available to the enquirer and the advantages and disadvantages of each option.
- apply reality testing strategies and problem solving strategies to achieve the best possible outcome for the Enquirer.
- remain impartial and communicate in a nonjudgmental manner.

Knowledge

Extensive knowledge of all aspects of workplace policies on conflict and resolution processes is required by a contact officer, and include:

- a working knowledge of what workplace bullying, sexual harassment and unlawful discrimination is, and what it is not.
- a working knowledge of the effects of workplace bullying on targets and the effects of allegations on complaint respondents.
- a comprehensive knowledge of the organisation's workplace bullying, harassment and discrimination policy and complaints procedure.
- a good understanding of what mediation entails, as well as its advantages and disadvantages.
- a good understanding of what a formal investigation process entails, as well as its advantages and disadvantages.
- a good understanding of the advantages and disadvantages of taking a complaint to an external jurisdiction.

Lack of resources, and failure of organisations to support contact officers once they are appointed, is one of the major criticisms of the contact officer role. It is important that contact offices are supported by HR, senior management, and their own manager. Contact officers that are not supported cannot effectively do their job, and may be at risk of victimisation themselves. This support means regular meetings, in-service education, peer support and managerial support. It is also important that the organisation gives the contact offices the time off during the periods needed to carry out their role. At times contact officers might find themselves in an ethical dilemma if there they are supporting a target who is complaining about a senior manager or someone known to them in the organisation. There needs to be someone in HR who the contact officer can speak to about these issues, and can take over their role if required.

The contact officer training course can be a 'stand-alone' course such as the one outlined below, or can incorporate a communication skills component, and/or a component for working with high conflict and high levels of emotion. Most of the state anti-discrimination or equal opportunity commissions offer contact officer training, although typically these are limited to information on sexual harassment and discrimination and do not include workplace bullying information.

The learning objectives of a typical contact officer training course are:

• for participants to acquire a sound understanding the role of the contact officer, and the limitations of the role

• to understand the complaint handling system available to employees including the key personnel, support persons such as an identified HR consultant and methods used by the organisation to identify, monitor and address risks

• to understand what is meant by 'confidentiality' and what they need to do if they are concerned about the safety of an enquirer, including who to contact

• to have a working knowledge of what is meant by unlawful discrimination, sexual harassment and bullying

• to understand the risk factors that contribute to workplace bullying and sexual harassment within an organisation

• to understand the difference between workplace bullying and reasonable management direction

• to understand what is meant by *mediation*, and what occurs during an *investigation* process

• to be familiar with the complaint handling options in the organisation's anti-bullying policy and complaints procedure, and a good understanding the advantages and disadvantage of each option for employees.

Endnotes

1 Reber, A., & Reber, I. (2001). *The Penguin dictionary of psychology* (3rd ed.). London, England: Penguin.

2 *McKibbin v South Australia (Office of the Public Trustee)* [2004] SAEOT 1

3 *Sluggett v Commonwealth of Australia* [2011] FMCA 609

4 *McKibbin v South Australia (Office of the Public Trustee)* [2004] SAEOT 1

5 Liefoogh, A., & Mackenzie-Davey, K. (2003). Explaining bullying at work: Why should we listen to employee accounts? In S. Einarsen, H. Hoel, D. Zapf, & C. Cooper (Eds), *Bullying and emotional abuse in the workplace: International perspectives in research and practice.* London, England: Taylor & Frances.

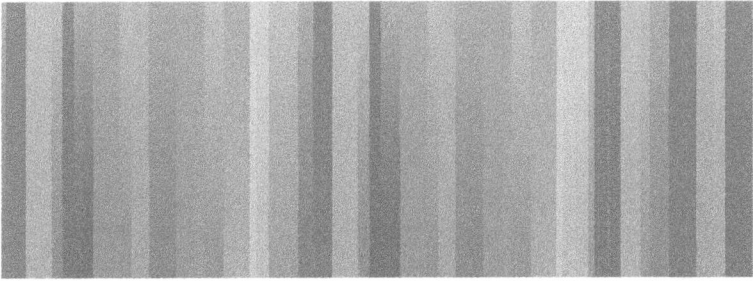

PART 4

When Things Go Wrong

CHAPTER 9

Levels of Intervention

Addressing the Complaint

Sometimes, despite the best planning, system design and implementation, a complaint of bullying or sexual harassment will be made. A spike in complaints often occurs when an organisation has begun to promote a new policy and undertake an awareness and training program. Because these strategies are being put into place, employees become more aware of their rights, and conflicts that have been simmering away in the background for a while may come to a head. People may feel that they are now able to safely complain about behaviours that they previously were hesitant to speak up about. Complaints may also arise when previously accepted behaviours in isolated departments or workgroups are challenged as being inappropriate.

When a complaint is made, it is important that it is taken seriously and addressed quickly. All complaints, whether they are verbal or written, must be addressed because they represent a potential workplace hazard. Employees may describe a range of experiences as 'bullying'. However, even if the behaviour has not reached the threshold of bullying as defined, if left unchecked, it has the potential to escalate into bullying. Therefore, all complaints need to be followed up. A complaint of bullying, whether it is substantiated or not, also means that there is behaviour occurring that is contributing to the complainant feeling disempowered or threated. It is a sign that something is wrong. Do not wait for a conflict to become bullying before you act.

COMPLAINTS — WHAT YOU MUST DO

- Document all actions you have taken to address the complaint.
- Follow up with all parties that the behaviour is no longer occurring.
- Document that you have followed up with the parties.

FOLLOW UP — DOCUMENT — FOLLOW UP — DOCUMENT
FOLLOW UP — DOCUMENT

When things go wrong, an organisation may need to intervene on a number of levels. Inappropriate behaviours may need to be addressed with the individuals involved as a performance management issue. Managers may want to facilitate a discussion or between both parties at a relationship level to address the behaviour or try to resolve a conflict. Following, an investigation of a bullying allegation, there may need to be intervene at a team or departmental level to address both the risk factors that have contributed to the bullying or to address the impact of an investigation or long standing conflict on the team. It is important that all interventions are undertaken by a qualified person who has the skills to sensitively address the issues that arise. It is also important that these interventions are part of an ongoing monitoring and risk management approach to preventing future inappropriate behaviours that could escalate into bullying or harassment.

Responding to an Initial Complaint

Talk through the issue with the complainant. If the issue is not serious bullying, but a low grade dispute or conflict, provide the complainant with resources to assist them to address the behaviour themselves if they feel safe to do so. Offer the complainant the opportunity to participate in conflict coaching in order to gain skills in managing and working through the conflict with the other party in a manner that might be more likely to resolve the problem. It is vitally important to follow up with the complainant after the conflict coaching to see if you can do anything further to assist them. It is not helpful to refer the complainant to counselling and then take no further action. This serves to

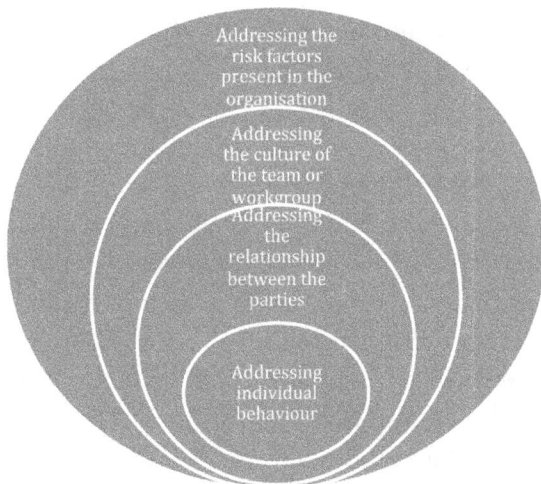

Figure 9.1
Levels of intervention..

reinforce that somehow they are at fault and no action will be taken by management, except to send them to counselling. While it may be appropriate to offer a distressed employee counselling, it is vital that managers follow up and takes steps to stop the behaviour that contributed to the complaint, if it is continuing. At the same time, keep an eye out for the poor behaviours described by the complainant. If you witness inappropriate behaviours, you *must* act. You cannot wait for another complaint, because managers have a duty of care to prevent potentially hazardous behaviours from occurring.

Inappropriate behaviour can also be addressed at a team level by reminding team members of their rights and responsibilities in relation to professional behaviour. Ask one of the organisation's contact officers to make a short presentation to the team following your next staff or toolbox meeting. Provide staff members with a copy of the organisation's 'Respectful Behaviour Policy'. Many teams have an item on their staff meeting agendas that deal with OH&S issues. This is a good opportunity to discuss psychological safety and remind all staff about their obligations in maintaining a safe workplace.

Managers are also encouraged to 'nip the problem in the bud' and act early on bad behaviours and unhealthy conflict's. Managers need to act early to address bad behaviours that are occurring. Low-grade rudeness or intimidating behaviours can escalate and become bullying if not nipped in the bud quickly. All discussions about inappropriate behaviours should be followed up ensure that the alleged behaviours are not continuing. Document that you have spoken to each party and follow up any interventions that you make.

Managers who have received complaints against them might be assisted by conflict coaching or management coaching in order to assist them to understand how they are perceived by staff. This will provide them an opportunity to change their style of interaction, which may be perceived as abrasive. While these managers may not intend to bully, an abrasive management style, and an overly defensive manager will find very difficult to see their actions from the perception of a staff member who is feeling threatened and disempowered. As such, a cycle of escalating conflict can build up with a manager becoming increasingly aggressive as they try to protect their image and justify their actions. This can result in bullying. An abrasive manner used by managers can contribute to highly stressed employees, and will be perceived as bullying if not addressed. Engaging in a coaching program to address this defensiveness may be helpful in 'taming the abrasive manager'.[1]

If complaints are not able to be successfully addressed through these initial steps, mediation may be appropriate. Even after an investigation, mediation allows both parties to talk together about what occurred and reach a resolution. Mediation allows both parties to express how the behaviour has impacted on them and also to be able talk about their perceptions of the issue. A mediated outcome need not replace any formal disciplinary action the organisation might impose following an investigation. Restorative mediation may be carried out following an investigation (and disciplinary action) in order to address the emotional issues that are not dealt with in a formal investigation, and also to focus on the future relationship between the parties. Mediation allows the parties involved in a complaint to talk freely about the issues in a safe, supported and confidential environment. Often the parties have been told not to talk to each other during an investigation, or following allegations of bullying, sexual harassment or discrimination. Therefore, the mediation is the first opportunity either party has had to express their views or explain their perspective. Mediation conducted from within an OH&S framework (see chapter 10) can also help identify risk factors within the organisation or department that contributed to the complaint and subsequent interventions that might prevent further unprofessional behaviours from occurring.

If high levels of team conflict or an inappropriate workgroup culture are identified as risks that have contributed to the allegations, there may need to be intervention at the team level. Intervention at this level needs to be specific to the risks that have been identified. For example, diversity training may be an appropriate intervention for teams in which marginalised workers are at risk of harassment or bullying. Teams that have had significant changes implemented may need an emphasis on change management, communication or policy development in order to take into account the impact of the changes on the way the work is undertaken. Team-building days can help workgroups overcome the division that allegations and investigations into bullying or harassment allegations have caused. Team debriefing after an investigation that is followed by team-building exercises with a focus on the future can assist teams to become a cohesive unit with a shared vision. Other interventions might specifically address team behaviours in relation to the organisation's code of conduct and respectful behaviour policy.

Organisational psychologists and conflict management specialists can help develop and facilitate group programs that focus on conflict resolution skills, promote team cohesion, increase resilience or help teams manage significant changes. Once again, follow up of these interventions is important to ensure that all team members are adhering to agreed codes of conduct and shared values.

At an organisational level, it is important to link respectful behaviour policies and complaints procedures with other workplace policies such as the organisation's OH&S policy, performance management policy, return-to-work policy or recruitment policy. These policies set standards of behaviour and directives that join the different areas of organisational life.

Endnote

1 Crawshaw, L. (2010). Coaching abrasive leaders: Using action research to reduce suffering and increase productivity in organisations. *International Journal of Coaching in Organisations, 29,* 60-77.

CHAPTER 10

To Mediate or Not to Mediate?

The Mediation Debate

Mediating workplace bullying, sexual harassment and discrimination complaints is a contentious issue, and there is a lively debate whether mediation is an appropriate intervention. Some of the arguments against mediating these types of complaints include:

- Bullying, sexual harassment and discrimination involve a misuse of power, so the parties in the mediation are not equals and there is an inherent power imbalance.

- Mediators focus on present and future relationships, so past behaviour is not addressed.

- Mediation does not determine facts, so bullying cannot be 'proved' through mediation.

- Mediation is a confidential process, so inappropriate behaviours that may be openly discussed during mediation are not addressed by the organisation.

- Mediation can serve to drive the inappropriate behaviour underground so it becomes more covert.

- There is often a lack of follow up and accountability of settlement agreements.

However, the main reasons why mediation is often rejected by complainants and respondents alike are

- unfamiliarity with the process of mediation
- a ridged perception of a win–lose approach
- high levels of emotion that block or distort communication
- a mistaken belief that entering into mediation is an indication of culpability.

Despite these potential problems, mediation is one of the most common strategies used to address discrimination and harassment. Mediation is a very common intervention in all sorts of disputes, including family court disputes, small business disputes and industrial disputes. When discrimination or sexual harassment complaints are lodged through external regulatory authorities such as state anti-discrimination bodies or the Human Rights Commission, very few complaints make it to court. This is because the first thing these agencies do after assessing the complaint is attempt to resolve the issues through conciliation (which is effectively mediation within a legal framework).

Many governments in western countries, including Australia and New Zealand, are moving closer and closer to making mediation and other alternative dispute resolution (ADR) processes mandatory prior to entry into the judicial system. Even in the area of family law and divorce (where there are significant power imbalances), mediation is compulsory prior to court.

If mediation is the *only* intervention into a complaint of workplace bullying, sexual harassment or discrimination, the mediation may act as a 'Band-Aid' that covers up some of the wider issues (risk factors) that have contributed to the alleged behaviour. If the sources of the alleged bullying are not addressed, risk factors that contributed to the conflict will continue. The OH&S model of mediation takes into account the sources of bullying

> While recommending mediation as an intervention in most workplace bullying complaints, if mediation is the only intervention used, it may do more harm than good and is not appropriate. Mediation is *not* recommended for *serious* bullying complaints.

and harassment, and aims to address these risk factors, as well as the relationship between the parties.

Mediation is NOT recommended for serious complaints. Serious bullying complaints are those where:

- The alleged perpetrator is a senior manager and the complainant is a base grade employee
- The alleged bullying has gone on for a long time
- There are multiple complaints against one alleged perpetrator
- When the alleged behaviour potentially constitutes a criminal offense

An OH&S Approach to Mediation

The OH&S approach to mediation doesn't just limit itself to addressing the issues between the parties, but it goes further and with the help of the parties involved in the conflict, the mediator identifies the background risks that may have contributed to the dispute. This approach uses the pre mediation intake assessment to explore the sources of the conflict and utilises the knowledge and experiences of the parties to identify background factors that may have contributed to the alleged behaviours. This broader assessment is carried out through the use of climate surveys, and in-depth interviews with the parties. Parties are informed that this information about the potential sources of the conflict is not confidential, but will be provided to HR in order that the background risk factors that may have contributed to the issues are addressed. This is made explicit and is written into the agreement to mediate. However, what is discussed during the mediation itself and the personal aspects of the conflict remain confidential.

During the final stages of the mediation, a senior manager or HR consultant is invited to join the parties as they finalise any settlement agreement reached. It is the job of this senior member of staff to follow up that the agreement is being adhered to by both parties, and neither is being victimised or subjected to further inappropriate behaviours. Because the dispute is a workplace dispute it is reasonable that a senior manager sign off and agree to any outcomes reached by the parties.

Following the mediation the mediator, recommends interventions to address some of the risk factors identified as contributing to the dispute. These interventions may include facilitated discussions between the parties, as well as team level interventions, or interventions specifically designed to address individual needs.

When Is Mediation Not Appropriate?

Mediation is not appropriate as an intervention into workplace conflict or bullying allegations in the following circumstances:

- When the issue involves a legal matter that only an investigation or court can decide;
- Where mediation is used as a forum to decide the substance of a complaint;
- When one party is in (physical or psychological) danger;
- When the allegation is serious and could be a criminal offence (e.g, allegations of assault should not be mediated but reported to the police);
- When there is a substantial power difference in the ability of either party to negotiate an outcome, and this difference cannot be balanced by the mediator or through third-party intervention;

- When the organisation does not want to address the background factors that contributed to the allegations, and mediation is the only intervention utilised;
- When there had been a history of multiple complaints against the same respondent;
- When there is unreasonable complaint behaviour present and the complainant is obsessively pursuing a minor matter in an inappropriate manner.

ARE YOU HAVING MEDIATION?

Here is a checklist of things to consider if you are having mediation.

- You should be able to bring a support person with you.
- Get to know your mediator. Ask the mediator lots of questions about the process and what to expect.
- What do you need to happen for the issues to be resolved?
- What do you think the other person needs to see happen for the issues to be resolved from their perspective?
- If mediation does not work, what other options do you have? What other options does the other person have? What are the advantages and disadvantages of each of these options for you and for them?
- What is the most realistic outcome that you might be able to achieve?
- What is the most realistic outcome you can expect from the other person?
- What needs to occur for each party to be able to work together professionally and respectfully in the future?
- What was happening in the work environment that contributed to the conflict?

Premediation

The premediation stage is an important part of the process as it prepares the parties for the mediation itself, and provides a framework for what is going to happen during and after the mediation. This stage is also very important in the OH&S model of mediation, as it is where the assessment of the sources of the conflict occurs. Some important aspects of premediation include:

- building rapport with the parties
- preparing a safe environment for the parties to discuss their concerns
- ascertaining whether mediation is a suitable intervention
- balancing power between the parties
- identifying the background sources of the alleged conduct, i.e risk factors that may have contributed to the issues in dispute
- establishing the limitations and extent of confidentiality.

HR professionals and mediators should not assume that the complainant and respondent want to mediate the issue. Mediation is a daunting experience for both parties. Most people are not familiar with the process, and there are many myths about what mediation is and what occurs behind the 'closed doors'. Complainants may be scared that they will have to face the alleged perpetrator without support, and respondents may feel defensive and see an agreement to mediate as a sign of culpability. Both parties will have high levels of emotion and may be experiencing anxiety and doubt. They may not trust the organisation or the process.

Because of these concerns, the premeditation stage is one of the most important parts of the mediation process. In this phase, the mediator needs to establish rapport and trust with both parties and educate them about the mediation process and what to expect from it, including single and joint sessions, confidentiality and the limits of confidentiality. It is also important that both parties know that the mediator's role does not extend to that of a judge or decision maker. The primary role of the mediator is to help both of the parties to resolve the issues.

In an OH&S model of mediation, the premediation stage takes longer than other types of workplace mediations. Where there have been allegations of bullying, sexual harassment or discrimination, the mediator might meet with both parties two or three times before bringing them together. Both parties may need conflict coaching or a number of one-to-one sessions with the mediator, prior to the mediation.

During the premediation sessions, both parties can help the mediator identify factors in the organisation's environment that they think contributed to the alleged behaviour. Taking a systemic approach is important, as there are often multiple factors that may be contributing to the allegations. The sources of the conflict or the alleged bad behaviours may occur on an individual level, team level and organisational level, and if not addressed may contribute to further or ongoing conflict after the mediation. The assessment of these factors can be carried out using specific tools such as premediation climate surveys or standardised psychometric instruments. However, exploring the perspective of each of the parties in the mediation is an important part of this assessment process. Identifying risk factors that contributed to the allegations is an important factor in ensuring that the conflict does not re-emerge once a mediated resolution has been reached. If potential risk factors that are present in the workplace environment are not addressed as part of a systemic intervention, there is a good chance that any settlement reached at mediation will not be sustainable.

If the conflict has reached the stage where one party continues to threaten and intimidate the other, mediation may not be possible. However, it may not be the alleged bully who is behaving in a threatening manner. I can recall a mediation where the complainant (the supposed target), displayed hostile, threatening and inappropriate behaviour towards the alleged bully and refused to acknowledge that their own behaviour may have been intimidating. In that particular case, the mediation was called off and the allegations formally investigated.

Conflict management coaching can be very helpful during the premediation phase. Conflict management coaching is an individual coaching process that assists both parties to examine the dispute from a number of different perspectives, and find ways in which they might be able to resolve the issues. Conflict management coaching can encourage each person to examine their own behaviours in a nonadversarial environment and help them gain insight into why their behaviours are perceived as abrasive or threatening, or how their retaliatory behaviours may have contributed to escalating the conflict. Conflict management coaching also assists the participant to examine different ways of resolving the dispute and the advantages and disadvantages of each alternative solution. During premediation coaching, the parties may be able to work with the conflict coach/mediator to address ways to accomplish their mediation goals.

Although most mediators would like to see a balanced power relationship between disputants, this type of relationship is not the norm in *any* mediation. Therefore, one of the primary roles of the mediator is to manage the power relationships between the parties irrespective of whether the issue has been labelled bullying by one of the parties. Some of the ways in which this can be done during the premediation sessions are through ensuring that both parties have support, are aware of their rights and are familiar with the mediation process. Other strategies, such as reality testing the options available should the mediation not work, can also assist in balancing the power differences. In most organisations, complainants who choose mediation as a complaint handling option are able to have the complaint investigated if the mediation is unsuccessful or the conflict continues following mediation.

In countries that have OH&S legislation that includes psychological hazards such as workplace bullying, targets also have the option of lodging a formal complaint with a regulatory authority outside the organisation. If the bullying involves sexual harassment or other behaviours that target an employee's specific attributes, such as their race, age, sex or disability, to name a few, they may also be able to lodge a sexual harassment or discrimination complaint with the relevant equal opportunity or anti-discrimination authority. Informing both parties of these options is one way of balancing the power between them.

Premediation Risk Assessment/Climate Survey

As a part of managing workplace bullying from an OH&S perspective, a premediation climate survey can provide the organisation with information about the workplace culture and factors that may have contributed to the conflict. An example of a premediation climate survey is provided at the end of this chapter. It is made clear to the mediation participants prior to carrying out this assessment that their answers are *not* confidential and will be passed on to the HR department. The climate survey responses, and subsequent discussion with the participants may inform part of the mediators recommendations to the organisation. The themes that are identified in the climate survey will inform the strategies that the organisation implements following the mediation, to help prevent similar issues from arising in the future. These strategies are control measures that an organisation carries out in order to manage identified risks that could contribute to bullying and harassment emerging as a problem.

Mediation

The mediation usually follows a set format, and significant phases include:

- Mediators opening remarks, restatement of ground rules and introduction to the session.

Pre meditation meetings

Focus on the past

1. Opening remarks by mediator.

2. Brief opening statement by each party, outlining main issues the in dispute. Mediator helps define issues and sets an agenda.

3. Expansion, exploration, and discussion of agenda items.

4. Confidential private sessions with each party to discuss concerns in the first part of the mediation and options for resolution including strengths and weaknesses of each option.

5. Options for resolution, and negotiation of settlement agreement.

6. Inclusion of HR representative to endorse final agreement.

Focus on the future

Post mediation follow-up

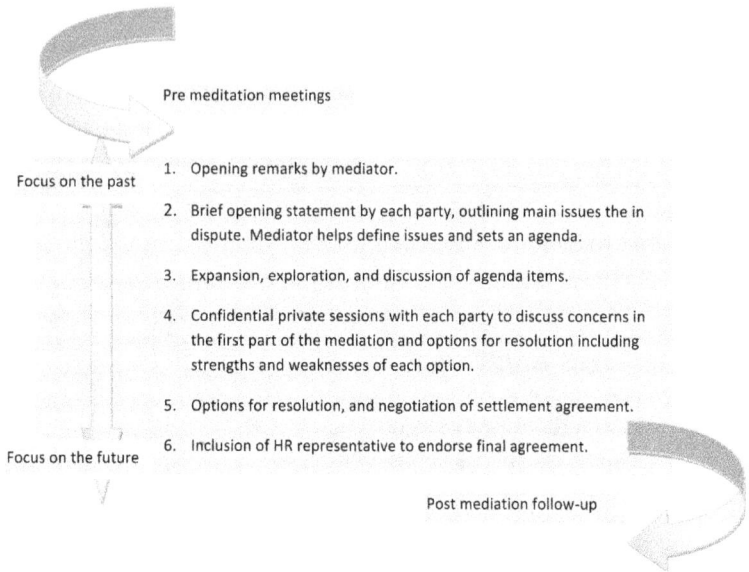

Figure 10.1
Phases of mediation.

- Each party's opening account of the issues, giving a broad overview (approx. 5 minutes in duration) of the problems that led to the mediation and their current perspective.

- From this overview, specific matters for discussion are identified and placed on a written agenda (usually on a whiteboard).

- Each issue is explored more fully and discussed in-depth.

- Confidential one-to-one sessions are held with the individual parties.

- A return to the joint session and a focus on the future and negotiation of an agreed resolution to the issues.

- A specific settlement agreement is developed.

- The final settlement agreement is finalised in conjunction with a senior manager or HR representative who joins in the mediation at this point in time.

At the beginning of the mediation session, the mediator usually makes an opening statement, restating ground rules (i.e., one person speaks at a time, the importance of and the limits of confidentiality), once again outlining the mediation process. Following a brief outline of each party's concerns, the mediator encourages both parties to contribute to an agenda so that each issue can be explored more fully. In this way both parties are able to have topics that are important to them noted and discussed.

Usually the first part of the mediation focuses on the exploration and discussion of issues that have been placed on the agenda. While the parties are encouraged to talk to each other about their perspective, the mediator asks questions that help clarify the issues raised and help them understand each other's perspective.

During the confidential private sessions, the mediator can address specific concerns of the individual party and discuss the various options for agreement and how they might like to resolve the issues. Private sessions can be used to brainstorm options for resolution, and the benefits and risks associated with each option. The mediator might also ask each party what might occur if they are unable to reach an agreement or resolution, what this would mean for them.

When the parties return after the private sessions, the focus is on the future. At this point, each party puts forward ideas to resolve the dispute and the mediator assists them to negotiate a settlement agreement.

The Settlement Agreement

When workplace bullying, sexual harassment or discrimination complaints are the focus of the mediation, I inform the parties that an HR consultant or a senior manager will be present during the final phase of settlement, when the written agreement is fine-tuned and documented. This is because the mediation and conflict has occurred in a workplace context, so the workplace needs a representative to endorse the agreement, and authorise any actions that have organisational implications. Agreements for training, conflict management-coaching, reinstatement of any leave, or transferring one of the parties to another area cannot be sanctioned without the authorisation of an organisation representative. It is also the role of the senior manager/HR consultant to make sure that both parties adhere to the settlement agreement. While the mediation itself and the discussions during the mediation including the presenting issues and preliminary development of the settlement agreement are confidential, a senior manager/HR consultant needs to sign off on the final agreement for the reasons outlined previously.

Postmediation Follow Up

Follow up after the mediation is important from an OHS framework in order to address the ongoing emotions and potential conflict between the parties as well as carrying out intervention into any OHS issues/risk factors identified as contributing to the allegations.

Identifying the risk factors and reporting them extends the traditional role of the mediator so that they are working as part of the HR 'team'. The factors identified as contributing to the conflict or allegations will inform postmediation interventions might take place at an individual, relationship, team and/or organisational level. At each level, these factors can include:

- Individual Level
  - Conflict coaching for individuals;
  - Management coaching;
  - Training in managing performance/dealing with high-conflict staff;
  - Skill development for individuals in an identified area of need.
- Relationship Level

- Ongoing facilitated discussions between parties in conflict;
- Further mediation to address other issues identified;
- conflict coaching at a relationship level.

• Team Level

- Managing conflict as a team;
- Diversity training
- Preventing bullying and harassment training staff 'rights and responsibilities';
- Team building — developing values and team goals.

• Organisational Level

- Policy development;
- Developing an integrated conflict management system;
- Developing an organisation-wide strategy addressing respectful behaviours (preventing bullying and harassment);
- Training for HR staff or senior managers throughout the organisation on their responsibilities to prevent bullying and associated behaviours.

It is recommended that following the mediation, HR is provided with a report that includes a copy of the settlement agreement, an outline of the themes identified in the pre-mediation climate survey and a summary of any other organisational issues that may have contributed tothe bullying allegations or the conflict between the parties. Recommendations for interventions to address issues that may have contributed to the conflict or allegations are also included in this report, so that HR is able to take measures to control or better manage these risk factors that have been identified.

Premediation Climate Survey

Sometimes there are background factors in the workplace environment that contribute to conflicts that can escalate into complaints of bullying, harassment or discrimination and cause significant distress for all the people involved.

Because you are involved in such a complaint and are trying to resolve the issues through mediation, you are both in a position to help identify some of the things that may have contributed to the initial conflict, and why it has escalated to this point. The information that you provide on this form may be discussed further in mediation if you wish, and will be shared with HR to help them plan interventions that might prevent similar situations occurring again.

Please feel free to outline any other issues that you think may have contributed to the conflict between you. This information will be shared with the HR Department and may contribute to other intervention strategies being implemented if deemed appropriate.

Department_____

Name
(optional)_____

Please circle the number that best corresponds with your experiences. If you want to add further comment, please do so.

1. My job allows me to use my skills, knowledge and experience

(Yes/Unsure/No)

2. I have a clear understanding of my job role and responsibilities

(Yes/Unsure/No)

3. I have a clear understanding of the reporting relationships in relation to my job

(Yes/Unsure/No)

4. I feel competent in using the technology that is needed to perform my job

(Yes/Unsure/No)

5. I feel secure in my job (If answered No, please state why not)_____

(Yes/Unsure/No)

6. I am able to go to my manager for help if I have a problem
   (Yes/Unsure/No)

7. My manager provides me with support if needed
   (Yes/Unsure/No)

8. My manager is respectful to others in the team
   (Yes/Unsure/No)

9. I feel safe performing my job
   (Yes/Unsure/No)

10. I feel that I am picked on at work because of a personal characteristic (name that characteristic _____)
    (Yes/Unsure/No)

11. I have regular discussions with my manager about my work and role
    (Yes/Unsure/No)

12. I feel respected during those discussions
    (Yes/Unsure/No)

13. I feel like a valued part of the team
    (Yes/Unsure/No)

14. I work in a healthy environment
    (Yes/Unsure/No)

15. My colleagues are friendly towards me
    (Yes/Unsure/No)

16. My manager is committed to providing a safe and healthy workplace
    (Yes/Unsure/No)

17. I have had the training necessary to carry out my job well
    (Yes/Unsure/No)

18. Practical jokes are often carried out in this team

    (Yes/Unsure/No)

19. Sexual jokes and innuendos are common in this team

    (Yes/Unsure/No)

20. I work in a very stressful environment

    (Yes/Unsure/No)

21. There have been significant changes in my workplace

    (Yes/Unsure/No)

For those in a managerial positions

22. I am confident performing my job as a manager

    (Yes/Unsure/No)

23. I do my best to get along with all of the team, and consider them friends

    (Yes/Unsure/No)

24. I have a tough but fair management style

    (Yes/Unsure/No)

25. Over the last year I have undertaken training in managing workplace conflicts

    (Yes/Unsure/No)

26. Over the last year I have undertaken training in managing staff performance

    (Yes/Unsure/No)

27. Over the last year, I have undertaken training in regard to my management responsibilities in preventing and addressing workplace bullying, sexual harassment and unlawful discrimination

    (Yes/Unsure/No)

28. I can go to my own line manager if I have any concerns

    (Yes/Unsure/No)

29. I receive good support in my role as a manager

(Yes/Unsure/No)

Please expand on any of your answers in the survey, and outline any other background factors that you think may have contributed to the current concerns that you have. These factors may help identify what other interventions may be needed to ensure that the outcomes from mediation are sustainable.

_____

_____

_____

CHAPTER 11

Investigating Complaints of Bullying

Preparing for the Investigation Process

There may be a time when an allegation of workplace bullying, sexual harassment or discrimination warrants a formal investigation. A complaint does not have to be in writing before an organisation is obliged to act on it. A serious verbal complaint may warrant investigation.

Any investigation should be conducted in line with your organisation's workplace policy and accompanying complaints procedure. It is this document that will deliver a transparent methodology to which investigators, complainants and respondents can refer.

In order to prevent victimisation during an investigation process, it may be necessary to separate the complainant and respondent. The complainant should not be removed from their workplace unless they agree to this, as it can potentially be seen as victimisation. The organisation may need to remove the respondent. This needs to be carried out in a sensitive and supportive way, offering the respondent choices about whether to be relocated for a period of time, whether they would like to go home on full pay pending the outcome of the investigation, or whether they are able to take a special project elsewhere during the course of the investigation to remove them from the vicinity of the complainant. While the respondent is not in the workplace, it is important that they be kept informed of the process and reassured that until the outcome of the investigation is known, there is no presumption of culpability. Respondents need just as much support as complainants during an investigation.

A Case of Potential Victimisation?

> I went to see the HR manager … and she said, 'We will move you somewhere else'. She was trying to be supportive … However, I didn't want to go anywhere else. I loved my job. I got on with all of my teammates. I wasn't the problem. His behaviour was getting worse and worse, and I just wanted it to stop. No one was doing anything about it. She wanted to move me, thinking that then I wouldn't complain anymore … but he was the one that was behaving like that. Why did I have to go? (Maria, Administration officer)

Considerations Before and After the Investigation Process

There are several principles to consider that underpin the investigation process discussed below.

Confidentiality

Confidentiality means that only the people who are directly involved with the investigation are to be spoken to regarding the matter. All parties involved, including witnesses, are not to talk about the issues with their workgroup or any other people involved in the investigation except on a need-to-know basis. They are able to debrief and discuss the impact of the investigation with a professional counsellor, their treating doctor or psychologist. A person who is concerned about the safety of someone involved in the investigation is able to discuss their concerns with a manager or senior HR consultant.

Vexatious Complaints and unreasonable complainant behaviour

Complainants who knowingly lodge a false or misleading complaint should be subjected to disciplinary action. Complainants who knowingly make a vexatious or false complaint should also be disciplined. Vexatious complaints include, but are not limited to, those that are malicious, made as part of a pattern of bullying or made to annoy or intimidate the respondent.

Unusually persistent, or 'high conflict' complaints who are unrealistic in the outcomes they want, and who have little insight into their own inappropriate behaviour need to have this behaviour managed. These complainants exhibit behaviour that includes making multiple formal complaints about trivial matters, not accepting the decision or outcome of a complaint resolution/investigation process, aggressive and threating behaviour towards complaint handling staff and the other parties to a complaint, and making unrealistic and impractical demands upon the organisation. These type of complainants are very rare, their behaviour presents significant problems for organisations, and complaint handling staff. Having documented processes to manage querulous complaint behaviour is important as the behaviour of these complainants can become very litigious, and an organisation needs to manage this risk accordingly.

Victimisation

It is important that a complainant will not be treated unfairly or unreasonably by the organisation for lodging a complaint in good faith, even if the complaint is not substantiated. A complainant will not be relocated against their should, demoted or penalised in any manner for lodging a complaint. Even if a complaint is not substantiated, the complaint needs ongoing

WHAT WOULD YOU DO?

Imagine you are a senior HR consultant called in to address the case of an employee who has made a verbal allegation of workplace bullying and sexual harassment against her team leader. She alleges that he often pretends to masturbate in her presence, making a joke out of it when she complains. She said he makes demeaning comments about female colleagues and clients and repeatedly asks her to stay later than the other staff in the office to complete urgent work, despite knowing she needs to get home to her family. She said he yells at her and other staff when he is frustrated with them. On a couple of occasions, he has thrown objects at her and other staff. She said that she complained to her manager three weeks ago, and he said he would speak to the team leader but nothing has happened. She is very angry with the team leader and the manager and feels she is getting nowhere.

- What is the first thing you do?
- How would natural justice inform how you address this complaint?
- What are the risks to the organisation if the management of the complaint did not adhere to the principles of natural justice?
- The respondent is a relative of the CEO. How do you manage this?
- Do you address the manager's inaction? How do you do this?

support and assistance to integrate back into their team, and rebuild their relationship with the organisation.

The respondent should not be victimised either, but treated in accordance with fair standards and actions. Even if a complaint against a respondent is substantiated, it is important not to bully or treat the perpetrator in a way that could be perceived as threatening or intimidating. Organisations need to reprimand or discipline perpetrators according to recognised principles and standards.

Natural Justice

Natural justice is also known as procedural fairness, which underpins all investigations and disciplinary actions. It is the foundation upon which our legal system is built. All investigation processes must adhere to two main aspects of natural justice. The first is the right of the respondent to know what they are being accused of. This allows the respondent the right of reply to the accusation including the ability to defend their actions. It is important that the respondent be informed of all of the information on which the investigator is relying to make their determination. Included in this aspect of natural justice is the importance of giving the respondent adequate notice to reply to the allegations made against them.

The second rule of natural justice is that the investigator must not be biased. For this reason, it is recommended that the investigator be appointed from outside the organisation and be experienced in the investigation of complex issues such as workplace bullying.

Follow Up

After the investigation, it is important to follow up with both parties to see how they are coping. An investigation is a very stressful process for complainants, respondents and witnesses who give evidence. Postinvestigation team building and facilitated debriefing can prevent gossip, misinformation and ongoing conflict and unprofessional behaviours from contributing to division within the team.

Postinvestigation mediation from a restorative justice perspective, allows the complainant to discuss with the respondent the impact of their behaviour. Often the parties have been separated since the commencement of the investigation, and mediation allows direct communication for the first time in a supportive and controlled environment. Postinvestigation mediation also provides an opportunity for the respondent to hear about how their behaviour has affected the complainant, apologise for it and let the complainant what steps they are taking to address the behaviour. It may provide an opportunity for the parties to discuss their future working relationship and take some control by formulating an agreement that provides a sense of safety and resolution for them both. This mediated agreement may be quite separate from any disciplinary action the organisation has taken.

CHAPTER 12

Tips, Tools and Traps

Making a Complaint

Making a complaint of bullying, sexual harassment or discrimination is serious. Complaining about frivolous behaviour is also serious, and serial complaints about frivolous or trivial matters can be viewed as a form of bullying in themselves. However, if someone is treating you badly, it is important not to let that behaviour continue or escalate. My advice would be to examine your organisation's policy and complaints procedures and speak to a contact officer about your options. It is important not to react aggressively or impulsively, or to do anything that might make the situation worse.

While organisations are obliged to respond to verbal complaints of bullying, if the behaviour is serious, writing down what is happening and making a written statement can be helpful. A written complaint is less likely to be ignored or forgotten. However, it may escalate the anxiety you feel when the matter is investigated and addressed at a formal level. For this reason, make sure you have some good supports.

Tips for Targets

Here are some tips to assist in providing clear information to report incidents.

- Report the specific behaviours that are occurring, rather than labels. For example, do not say, 'My manager is bullying me'; rather, talk about specific behaviours that are actually happening or being exhibited.

- If you decide to make a formal written complaint, keep records of all documents pertaining to your allegations. Keep a copy of the original documents and provide a copy to HR.

- Avoid writing eight-page complaints, sending long, over explanatory e-mails, phoning every day to check on progress, or getting tied up in detail. This makes it very difficult for people who are trying to address the problem, and it can make them frustrated and less likely to approach you for clarification or assistance.

- Say what happened, not how it made you feel. Investigators will not be concerned about how it made you feel (mediation can address that), they will only be looking for evidence in regard to what allegedly occurred.

- In the first instance, try to have your concerns resolved through more sensitive and informal means. Ask your manager or HR consultant to help you resolve the matter. Mediation might also be an option to help you communicate effectively with the other person and examine ways of resolving the problem. If the behaviour is serious and you do not believe the organisation is taking your complaint seriously, mediation may not be appropriate.

- Mediation following an investigation can also be helpful in allowing you to talk to the other person about how their behaviour affected you and how you can both work together in the future.

- If your organisation does not have a policy or complaints procedure, there has been no training for staff or managers, and the bad behaviour is not addressed, get out. It is not worth staying in an unsafe environment if it is going to make you sick. If your workplace does not have a respectful behaviour policy or complaints procedures, and staff and managers have not had any training in the area, the bad behaviour will probably get worse. Ask for advice through your union, Working Women's Centre, OH&S regulator or anti-discrimination authority.

- If you make a complaint, be prepared for potential reprisal. While victimisation is prohibited by the law, it is rare for someone complaining about bullying, sexual harassment or discrimination not to face some recriminations. This is because often they are complaining about behaviour that has gone unchecked for some time, and their complaint is 'upsetting the apple cart'.

- A complaint to an external regulatory authority (such as an equal opportunity or anti-discrimination agency or an OH&S authority) is essentially an allegation that the organisation allowed the behaviour to occur. Your organisation will probably engage lawyers to defend their liability, and the matter will escalate. You might find yourself with little support at work. If you are going to complain outside the organisation it is recommended that you have good support and advocacy through your union, lawyer or Working Woman's Centre.

- Talk to someone. Do not suffer alone. Talk to your local doctor, EAP, union or psychologist.

Responding to an Allegation

Being accused of bullying, sexual harassment or discrimination can be very upsetting. It may mean that your behaviour has come across as defensive, abrasive or overly controlling. It may mean that your sense of humour has offended someone. You may not have intended to hurt or intimidate anyone, but your behaviour has been perceived as threatening and unreasonable. The law does not care if your behaviour was unintentional.

Tips for Respondents

Here are some tips to respond to allegations.

- Now is not the right time to get angry or aggressive. If you do not understand what the problem is, do not dismiss it. Rather, stop and think about the complaint from the other person's perspective.

- Talk to a colleague or someone who you know will give you honest feedback about your behaviour. The organisation's employee assistance program might be a good place to obtain some confidential and objective feedback about the way your behaviour is perceived.

- Letting the person who you have hurt or offended know that you are sorry and are taking responsibility for stopping the behaviour can go a long way to restoring the relationship.

- Conflict coaching might assist you to manage your frustrations and actions better. It will help you to understand how and why you have hurt someone, and assist you to acquire skills in addressing conflicts in a more constructive manner.

- Ask your HR department for assistance in addressing some of the issues that have been bought to your attention.

When we are under stress, we all have the potential to behave in a way that can be perceived as bossy, abrasive or threatening. It is important to consider how you behave when your ideas or behaviours are challenged or when you are placed in a stressful situation.

You may not be aware that your actions, attitude or behaviour has come across as threatening and has caused offence. Resolving issues informally and apologising for any distress you have caused can de-escalate conflicts and assist both parties to move forward. However, this apology needs to be genuine. An insincere apology, can escalate matters, especially if there is no change in your behaviour. If the complaint is about the way in which you manage staff or behave in conflict situations, you may benefit from conflict coaching or leadership mentoring. This can often be arranged through HR or an organisation's EAP. Many organisational psychologists and workplace mediators also provide management and conflict coaching.

Mediation can also be a useful method of resolving the issues. This is because the best way to resolve a conflict is usually by having the people directly involved, listen to and understand each other, and come up with solutions to the problem themselves. Mediation is not about blaming or attributing right and wrong, and the mediator's job is not to take sides or establish facts. The primary role of the mediator is to help the people involved in the conflict or dispute to listen carefully to each other and work out what the problem is, so that they can come up with ways of resolving the issue. If either party starts behaving badly in mediation, the mediator can stop the process and might talk to both parties about alternatives to mediation. Mediation is a confidential process, which means that without the permission of both parties, the mediator will not speak to anyone about what is discussed during the mediation (unless they think someone is in danger).

If the mediator uses the OHS model of mediation that is recommended in this book they will obtain your permission to report back to HR some of the background variables that may have contributed to the complaint. These might include high levels of team stress, lack of training or difficulties you have interacting with employees in a highly volatile climate. Knowing how these stressors have contributed to the complaint against you may mean that you

> ## ASK YOURSELF
>
> - Do I take my stress out on my staff or others in the department?
> - How do I treat others when faced with tight deadlines and increased work pressure?
> - Does my sense of humour offend anyone?
> - Are my actions sometimes perceived as inappropriate? Do I need to curb my behaviour?
> - Would my staff label me as abrasive when stressed?
> - Do I treat some employees better than others? Why?
> - If I do not like someone, how do I behave towards them? How might this be interpreted?
> - Do I motivate others through reward or punishment?
> - Do I ignore or exclude people at work whom I do not like?
> - How do I use my managerial power to get what I want? How might this be perceived by people with less influence than me?
> - How do I feel when criticised or challenged? How do these feelings manifest themselves in my behaviour? How might this affect others?
> - What are the different options I have to resolve this dispute? What are the short-term and long-term advantages and disadvantages of these options? Are there any other options that might help both of us move forward?

are better able to access training or coaching to address your contribution to the conflict. It may also mean that the team and the other people involved in the complaint are also assisted to address their contribution.

If a formal complaint has been made against you and the matter is going to be investigated, you have a right to know what the specific allegations are and who made the allegations against you. You have a right to tell your side of the story and to be heard. However, if the complaint against you is substantiated, the organisation has the right to discipline you. Serious allegations that are substantiated may result in termination of an employment contract. Workplace bullying, sexual harassment and unlawful discrimination is not just about bad manners. This behaviour poses a risk to the health of staff. These behaviours are illegal. Organisations cannot afford to have someone working for them who behaves in a way that potentially causes harm and invites litigation.

The Injured Employee

Workplace bullying and sexual harassment can result in psychological injury. A misguided investigation or mishandling of a complaint can exacerbate an injury and can alienate a vulnerable worker, contributing to further psychological harm. In Australia if an employee is injured at work, they may able to make a claim for workers compensation insurance for the leave required to recover from their workplace injury and for treatment expenses incurred as a result of the workplace injury. This type of leave is commonly referred to as 'stress leave' in relation to psychological injuries. A number of studies have found that the decision to lodge a stress leave claim following a workplace injury is influenced not only by the severity of the injury but by the claimant's relationship with co-workers,[1] as well as the organisation's response to the stressful incident and the claimant's perceptions of the organisational fairness.[2]

Helen Winefield and her colleagues conducted some interesting research into why some employees made workers compensation claims for psychological injury.[3] They found that negative perceptions of fairness — in particular, the perceived unfairness of workplace policies and procedures governing workplace decision making—were predictors of claiming for psychological injury. In this study, workers who felt helpless, who believed decisions were made unjustly, and who believed they were treated without respect were more likely to make a claim for psychological injury than those workers who believed that they had been treated fairly by the organisation. This finding supports a number of other studies that suggest a decision to lodge a workers compensation claim for psychological injury is contributed to by a lack of support from management and perceptions of unfairness in the way that management responded to the worker's grievance.

The following cited transcripts are from individual case studies that highlight the sense of unfairness that contributed to these complainants lodging a stress claim as a result of workplace bullying.

> First of all, I am 60 years of age. I have been in the workforce since I was 15, so effectively for 40 years I have never had a WorkCover claim. Never wanted one. So, I didn't want to take WorkCover as an option, and I refused it initially, but things escalated with the problems I was having at work to a point where I had no option. By this stage, I had really fallen apart and so I went back to my doctor and said, 'Now I have got to take WorkCover. I've got to because I am just not well, and I am not getting paid, and HR [the bully was the head of HR] is making it worse, and I have to do something. (Rhyse, Senior Manager, Private Industry)

As illustrated by Rhyse's transcript, applying for workers compensation was viewed as a last resort, as he prided himself on having never made a workers compensation claim in his 40-year working life. He reported that he only applied for stress leave as a last resort when the organisation would not act on his complaints and he 'had no option' because he had 'fallen apart'.

This theme of injustice also preceded Nora's decision to lodge a WorkCover claim:

> Hence, the CEO just totally 100 per cent stuck up for (sic) … Never even asked me one question about the incident, never asked me how loud she had screamed, what it was over or anything. He showed absolutely no concerns for me that I had been verbally abused … They didn't care about how I felt or what I had gone through … and I walked out and went off to the doctor and got a WorkCover certificate. (Nora, Administration Assistant, Not for Profit Agency)

Nora's transcript describes the link between taking out a stress claim and believing that the CEO did not care about her. It also reveals her sense of unfairness and injustice. John described a similar situation:

> I think the people who were the perpetrators knew that they were getting away with it. So, I think to me it just seemed as though they were going to continue with this behaviour until I had to put in a stress claim. By the time they dealt with it, things had gotten so out of hand that I had actually left. I had actually gone on stress leave. (John, Public Servant)

From John's perspective, the perpetrators would continue to 'get away with' the behaviour until he put in a stress claim and it was recognised as being inappropriate behaviour.

The strong message to organisations from these studies is twofold. First, it is important to protect your workers from behaviours that may potentially contribute to stress-related injuries. This book has highlighted the steps that employers can take to assess and control risks in their workplace that might contribute to these sorts of injuries. The second point is that if inappropriate behaviour occurs, it is potentially harmful to a worker and needs to be addressed immediately. Workers need to know that their organisation is supporting them and cares for their wellbeing. If a worker believes that their complaint is not being taken seriously or that they are being treated unfairly by the organisation, they will be much more likely to make a claim and take stress-related leave.

Tips for HR Professionals:

The following tips may assist HR professionals.

- Treat all complaints seriously — they will not go away.
- Address the complaint in a systemic manner. Do not just focus on the target and perpetrator (individual level) but assess and deal with the background variables that contributed to the complaint.
- Be seen by all staff to be serious.

- Follow up regularly with the target to see how they are managing.
- Ask the target what support they need.
- Be flexible in your approach.
- Be aware that workers who are anxious, depressed, angry or distressed may not always act rationally or appropriately. They have a psychological injury/illness. These workers may at times cope in a way that is counterproductive. People with depression or anxiety may perceive neutral events as antagonistic and may be defensive or super-sensitive. Be flexible in your approach and reinforce appropriate behaviours and coping strategies within a supportive environment. As workers with a psychological injury may have poor memory and concentration, they will need reminders, follow up and support.
- Do not send distressed workers off to counselling and then cease contact with them. They will perceive this as abandonment.
- Use your respectful behaviour policy and complaints procedures to guide you.
- Ensure that your actions are transparent and adhere to the principles of fairness and justice.
- Document all of your actions and follow up.

Myths and Facts About Bullying and Harassment

There are a number of myths about workplace bullying and sexual harassment. These are perpetuated through ignorance, and poor knowledge about what bullying and sexual harassment actually is. However, they can be challenged through explaining bullying and sexual harassment in a logical and accurate manner. The following myths and facts can be used as a training tool to stimulate discussion and highlight how myths in regard to workplace bullying and harassment can do more harm than good.

Myth	Fact
Workplace bullying is really just a personality clash, and if left alone, the people involved will sort it out.	Workplace bullying is not just a personality clash. Workplace bullying is repeated threatening or intimidating behaviour that has the potential to harm someone. Because bullying involves the misuse of power by the perpetrator, and the subjugation of a target, If left alone, there is the risk of sustaining a psychological injury.
Bullying and sexual harassment complaints are over reported and are not as big a problem as they appear.	While sometimes behaviours that do not meet the criteria for bullying are reported, a lot of bullying and sexual harassment is under reported because of fear of retribution or victimisation. Organisations that have poor reporting systems or where managers do not act to stop bullying or sexually inappropriate behaviours at work contribute to the under reporting of these behaviours. When senior staff engage in bullying or sexually inappropriate behaviour many targets see no point in reporting the behaviour because they know they will not be taken seriously. Many targets do not report bullying or sexual harassment because they are embarrassed. Many fear losing their job if they report the behaviour. Some targets do not report bad behaviour because they do not know their rights1
If my manager tells me off, he/she is bullying me.	Managers are allowed to performance manage employees. Sometimes this may involve stern words, and warnings. However if the performance management is carried out in a respectful manner, feedback is fair and is justified, it is not bullying.
It is the job of the employer to stop workplace bullying.	It is the job of *all staff* to prevent workplace bullying. The employer is responsible for carrying out all reasonable steps to prevent and manage bullying from a systemic perspective. However, *all* staff are responsible for behaving in a respectful and professional manner towards each other at all times. Managers have an added responsibility to prevent and address inappropriate behaviour that might develop into bullying, and witness to bullying have a moral obligation to speak out.
Managers can only act on a complaint of bullying or harassment if they are written down.	No. Managers need to act on all inappropriate behaviour if they see it. They also need to prevent and stop any behaviour that is potentially a psychological hazard. That means that if they see, or hear of behaviour that is potentially bullying, or sexual harassment they must act.

Myth	Fact
Managers are always the bullies, and the targets are their subordinates.	Research shows that managers can be bullied, by their staff, but are less likely to report the behaviour. Bullies are people who have power. While that may be managerial power it can also be power that is related to knowledge, length of tenure, culture, gender, sexuality and a number of other factors.
If I did not mean to offend someone, then I am not bullying or harassing them.	The bullying, sexual harassment and anti-discrimination laws do not take into account intention. Even if you did not mean to intimidate or offend someone; if you repeatedly behaved in a way that was perceived as intimidating and threatening, and a 'reasonable person' would have viewed your behaviour as intimidating and threatening, and possibly contributing to an injury, then you may be bullying. For sexual harassment and discrimination to occur, the offensive behaviour need only occur once.
If I tell someone, I will make it worse.	It is really important to report bullying. The research shows that unreported bullying becomes worse over time, and can lead to both physical and mental health problems. If you cannot talk to anyone at work, talk to your union, doctor, or a friend. Do not stay silent about behaviour at work that is making you feel frightened or sick.
Bullying is a normal part of 'tough' management, and makes employees work harder.	Bullying is not tough management, and employees who feel bullied are less productive, have more sick leave, make more mistakes and generally a team who feels bullied, has poor moral and less commitment to the organisation.
Preventing workplace bullying is more costly than addressing a complaint.	Few organisations actually calculate the cost of workplace bullying. However, bullying can contribute to increased costs through: • Poor productivity, • More mistakes made by the target, team members and witnesses, • Poor team moral, • Distrust of management, • High levels of absenteeism, higher staff turnover, increased costs in relation to sick leave, workers compensation / medical costs, • Costs involved in replacing staff who leave, • Increased insurance premiums, • Increased time investigating complaints • Costs involved with rehabilitating targets following psychological injury / stress leave.

Myth	Fact
	A bullying, sexual harassment or unlawful discrimination complaint to an external regulatory authority can incur additional costs through: • Legal fees, • Poor publicity for the organisation and individuals involved, • Time off work for all parties involved, • Costs involved in investigating and defending legal action, • Financial penalties for both the organisation, and individual perpetrators if complaint substantiated.
People who are bullied 'ask for it' and are overly sensitive.	Research has shown that there is no such thing as a typical 'victim personality'. Workers who are bullied can come from all areas within an organisation, including management. Many people who are bullied because they are different from the majority of people in the team. Often targets of bullying put up with bad behaviour for a long time before reporting it.
People who are bullied should be nice to the perpetrators and try to 'win them over.'	If someone is being bullied it does not matter what they do, the perpetrator will exert their power over them and treat them badly. The best thing that a target can do is tell someone. Use the organisations policy to guide you, or get some advice from your OH&S regulatory authority, Anti-discrimination agency, union, or mental health help line.
People who are bullied should 'fight back' and 'give as good as they get'.	Fighting back will only put a target in a worse position, and will serve to escalate the bullying. Do not retaliate. Document what is happening, and report the behaviour. If you fight back, then your own behaviour may get you into trouble.
Bullying is the same thing as conflict.	Bullying is not conflict. Bullying involves the misuse of power to intimidate, and subjugate a target. If not stopped, bullying escalates over time until the target becomes ill or leaves the workplace.
Sexual harassment only happens to women.	Sexual harassment more commonly occurs to women. However, men are also sexually harassed. Men may be more reluctant to report sexual harassment than women. Women can be sexually harassed by other women, and men can be sexually harassed by women or men.

Myth	Fact
Some people ask to be sexually harassed by dressing provocatively or acting flirtatiously.	Sexual harassment has nothing to do with how a person looks, how they act, dress or how old they are. No person irrespective of their age, sex, dress, sexuality or physical appearance should be subjected to unwelcomed sexual behaviour of any kind. If a person is acting unprofessionally, by wearing inappropriate clothing to work or behaving inappropriately, this needs to be addressed by management. There is no excuse for sexual harassment.

Endnote

1   Rosenman, K.D., Gardiner, J.C., Wang, J., Biddle, J., Hogan, A., Reilly, M.J., & Welch, E. (2000). Why most workers with occupational repetitive trauma do not file for workers' compensation. *Journal of Occupational and Environmental Medicine, 42*(1), 25–34.

2   Roberts, K., & Markel, K. (2001). Claiming in the name of fairness: Organisational justice and the decision to file for workplace injury compensation. *Journal of Occupational Health Psychology, 6*(4), 332–347.

3   Winefield, H., Saebel, J., & Winefield, A. (2010). Employee perceptions of fairness as predictors of workers' compensation claims for psychological injury: An Australian case-control study. *Stress and Health, 26*, 3–12.

www.ingramcontent.com/pod-product-compliance
Lightning Source LLC
Chambersburg PA
CBHW062020270326
41929CB00014B/2266